For those who walk paths they were never intended to walk

"Pain is real,
but so is hope."
-Tabitha McDuffee

"The discipline of creation, be it to paint, compose, write, is an effort toward wholeness."
-Madeline L'Engle, *Walking on Water: Reflections on Faith and Art*

INTRODUCTION

First, there is void.
Then, a voice:
a spark, an explosion, an illumination, a gathering of matter, a body molds from atoms, a neuron forms and fires

vibrant colors flash, soft sounds echo, harsh scents waft, bumpy textures rise, bitter tastes pucker—a soul breathes and stirs

Genesis 1:1, 2:7
In the beginning, God created the heavens and the earth . . . And the Lord God formed man of the dust of the ground, and breathed into his nostrils the breath of life; and man became a living soul.

THE COLOR OF PAIN

THE INTERSECTION OF MIGRAINE, ART, AND FAITH

A MEMOIR

ABBY J. REED

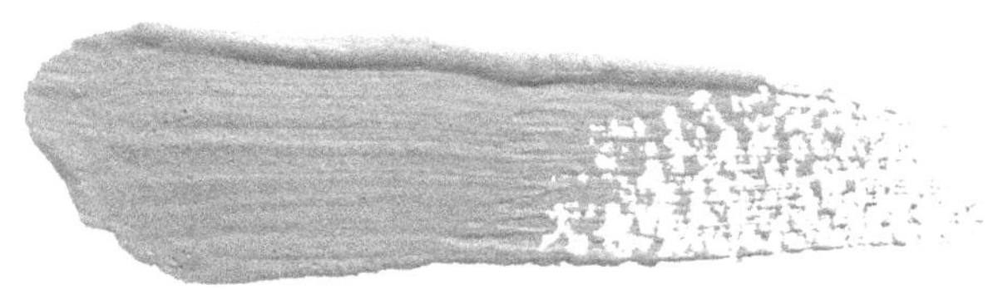

As this is a work of creative nonfiction, some names and identifying details have been changed to ensure the privacy of those involved, and time altered slightly. Events have been preserved to the best of the author's memory, which is inherently faulty, as the author's mother likes to continuously remind her.

1

I can tell you what this book is by first telling you what it's not.

This isn't a guide on how to abolish migraines and discover physical healing. This isn't a deep theological treatise with completely accurate and non-contradictory belief systems. This isn't a story about a creator who doggedly pursues their art without question.

This is, quite simply, the book I needed when my migraines were at their worst.

If you're looking for a messy life and a messy story that knots together art, faith, and pain in a semblance of meaning, I got you. If you're looking for honest questions with very few answers, well, you'll find plenty. If you don't mind contradictions because life is filled with them, then, please, hold my hand.

You don't have to walk this path alone.

2

I should mention: You'll find I use the word "pain" a lot. That's because, for me, the most disabling part of migraine is head pain. For others, it's nausea. Or brain fog. Or seizure-like-symptoms. And just because I focus on head pain, doesn't mean the rest of my body isn't experiencing some other symptom. Because migraine is not a headache. Headaches only affect the head, while migraine affects the entire neurological system, including causing light and smell sensitivity, nausea, tingles in the body, ringing in the ears, and more. Migraine is a full-body neurologic disease; it's a disability, chronic illness, invisible illness, etc.

It's also extremely common. As of writing this, The Migraine Research Foundation says that migraine is currently the sixth most disabling illness in the entire world, affecting over 9 million men and 28 million women in the US alone.

Those aren't numbers to sniff at.

Treating migraine usually takes a multipronged approach, which is why I don't discuss all the variety of my treatments over the years because there have been, are, and will be so many. I circulate between Western medication such as beta blockers, antipsychotics, and blood dilators, and more nontraditional routes such as massage, dietary choices, lifestyle management, therapy, great sunglasses, and back again.

While the Egyptians tied clay crocodiles to their foreheads to get rid of head pain, and the Sumerians wore headbands made from goat hair—and don't forget the Victorians who drilled holes in their skulls or locked their loved ones in horrid asylums—I've been advised to place banana peels on my forehead and even—my personal favorite—use daily coffee enemas. Which isn't as far-fetched as you might think. Caffeine can act as a painkiller when timed right, since it dilates the blood vessels. Thankfully, my grandma has faithfully sent me every possible cure for migraine seen on infomercials and Facebook ads for the last twenty years.

Even more thankfully, none of the celebrities with migraine have tried these more outlandish remedies. That I know of. I think we would've noticed if Elvis Presley or Serena Williams or Julius Caesar or John F. Kennedy walked around with clay crocodiles tied to their heads.

You'll also find I go back and forth with my diagnosis and never fully state or describe the specific type(s) of migraine I have. That's because my diagnosis has changed over the years; and it will probably change again. Migraine is considered a "moving target" disease. What helps one week may not help the next, and once you find a decent treatment plan, the darn thing evolves. There's not much research out there on migraine, and as understanding grows, so will our labels. Migraine has been around for thousands of years, yet nobody understands *precisely* how migraine works. Partly because it's traditionally been seen as a women's disease, and the surrounding stigma led to a lack of funding. *All in My Head* by Paula Kamen explores this topic of female hysteria in relation to both the medical field and migraine in depth.

Migraine is a mystery. But can any of us say exactly how God speaks or a how story sparks to life?

Life is filled with mysteries. Sometimes we're just asked to live with them.

PRODROME

The prodrome stage of a migraine can take place anywhere from a couple days to a week before the aura and headache begin. You often experience symptoms without realizing it. That random mood swing? Symptom. That stomach indigestion? Symptom. That sentence slipping from your thoughts? Symptom.

A creative project can begin hours to years before you realize you're building something. Your subconscious collects interesting data, images, snippets of dialogue long before your conscious self decides to begin.

Genesis 1:2
The earth was without form, and void, and darkness was on the face of the deep. And the Spirit of God was hovering over the face of the waters.

3

My mom says I had migraine attacks as early as kindergarten, probably even earlier, as though I came out of the womb with a migraine. Apparently I visited the nurse's office a couple times a month. I only remember trash cans and someone saying, "Again, Abby?" and a suspicion that the true reason I vomited behind the meanest teacher in school wasn't due to a stomach flu, but the pain in my head.

The first time I fully remember having a migraine attack is in fifth grade. A faint smell of chalk dusts the air, and math equations dance across the board. The classroom is stuffed with kids, and I have a worn sticker on my desk that says, *With God anything is possible.* I'm nearly ten, and it's the year I believe I can grow up to be a kangaroo and spend half the year hopping between lunch and recess. My husband says if he met me then, we never would've gotten together because I am too weird. I poke him and tell him, "We just would've gotten married in a kangaroo conservatory."

I stick my tongue between my teeth, grip my pencil, and scrawl my name across my oversized lined paper. My feet beat against the side of my desk.

The letters in my name disappear, like an invisible eraser follows my pencil lead.

I stop kicking.

I finish writing my name. My last name disappears too.

Colors shimmer where the letters used to be. As I watch, they turn into a vortex of shimmering rainbow lights to form a stunning C shape.

I gasp.

It's beautiful.

I turn around to my friend George. The C follows me. It mutilates part of his face, melting his features into a blur. I reach out to touch the form.

He jerks away. "What're you doing?"

"Don't you see that?"

"See what?"

I blink. The C is still there when I close my eyes. I turn back around and watch as the form travels across my paper, across the class, across the other kids in the room, growing until the colors eat my entire vision like a dream leaked into this reality. Then it fades into the edges of my sight, vanishing.

My memory is gone after that. The only leftovers are snippets of curling up with ice packs on the nurse's couch and tripping over someone's legs to vomit.

It doesn't take me long to associate the magical C shape

with pain. By junior high, the thing I'm most afraid of are my migraines.

The migraines are so much a regular part of my life by now that my routine is instinctive. If my parents are home, I announce the aura with a deadpan voice, usually to my dad, because he has a quieter presence. Every migraineur knows a quiet presence and a quiet voice makes a mecca. No drama needed or wanted. I march to the medicine cabinet, swallow medicine, then migrate to my parents' bedroom.

My parents have decorated in cool colors, while my bedroom is a sharp contrast of purple and white. It's unbearably hot by 8:00 a.m. because of the way my windows face the Californian sun, and Bakersfield is known for its 100+ degree weather. I hate trying to sleep after a migraine in the same bed that earlier cupped my pain. A separate migraine space, if possible, acts like a barrier that mentally helps prevent the pain from seeping into the rest of my life.

My parents' duvet cover and pillows are covered in a silky material. In migraine language, silk = cool = a godsend. Ten years later I discover ice packs. (One of the problems of having pain so young is that you might not know all the coping options and are so immersed in your routine you don't know there's another way.)

I close all the shades, turn the fan on high, and cover myself with a light blanket for weighted comfort.

And wait.

And wait.

Wait until the aura finishes marching across my vision, a kaleidoscope of flickering, metallic colors. In this season, the aura is always single C shape, growing out. Sometimes a single line rims the exterior of my vision—then grows *inward* until it vanishes.

A pause.

Silence.

If I'm lucky, I fall asleep. Most of the time, I'm not lucky.

The pain hits like a rubber mallet. At first soft yet firm, then building until the mallet transforms into a jackhammer. Sharp and unrelenting. Everything around me blurs.

I thrash against the sheets. The pain burns so fierce my tear ducts seem broken. I can't cry. The only way to get any sort of relief is to move and move and move against it. My legs jumble in the pillows and blanket. My dad walks past me drowning in the bed, toward his office. Does he see me? He has his own pain, though, and I don't blame him for not stopping, because I know what pain is like. Pain narrows the vision so the only thing you can see is this second, this moment, this now. You can't see outside yourself.

After several hours, the sharpness gives way to a softer pain. I stop thrashing and move to a rocking and humming. The sound of my voice vibrates against my skull, giving a small measure of relief. I can now wait out the rest of the hours, hungover, exhausted, too weak to move.

Eventually I fall asleep, letting the pain move to the back of my head where it becomes bearable.

After another four hours, I emerge from my cave and join the rest of my family to let the hangover finish its two-day course.

As I type now, a tightening notches in my chest. I'm

aware of the pain in my head. The vice grip it has on my brain. The way it both buries claws into the root of myself, yet also seems to skim along my skull. Like a living jellyfish floating along the surface of the ocean, with its tentacles dangling deeper. I skim through my journal entries from this time, expecting to find a righteous diatribe against migraine. Instead, they were so common I just wrote, *Migraine last night*, or, *Migraine today/yesterday*. Like I recorded the weather. As if they were the most expected and common thing in the world—because, to me, they were.

I think I learned from an early age that parents can't fix everything. Parents can't save you. Parents can't help you. Some things you can only deal with by yourself. This is a belief I take all the way with me into marriage. It's a common theme in my character arcs in my fiction.

As I finish typing this, the pain in my head lessens a bit. The iron claws stabbing my temple move backward, raking toward the rear of my skull, leaving a haunting echo vibrating next to my eyes. The movement allows me to breathe easier. Then the claws return to my temples, and I hunch over the keyboard, burying a knuckle against the spot. The pain could be from writing or the weather. I'm going to get up to drink some caffeine to see if that helps.

4

The aura starts in second period. The telltale flashing lights suck in the faces of my high-school classmates like a black hole. I don't even get the initial chill anymore, just a sickening sense of resolution, of giving in. I sigh and tuck my knees up against my desk, an advantage to having long legs, and sneak my phone out from my purse. It's one of those old phones with T9 texting. You really have to commit to a message to type it out.

Migraine. Pick me up?

Dad's working, so send to Mom.

I pack up my backpack, dry swallow some meds, let my temple touch the cool of the desktop. It's not as though I can see the board anyway. I slide my phone between my thighs and wait for the telltale vibrate. The aura has grown halfway across the room before my mom's reply comes.

I tip the screen toward me and squint, angling my head so I can read out of the one visible corner of my vision.

Can't. It would be 45 min to get you, 45 back, by that time I can't pick up your siblings . . .

The first wave of nausea hits, and I focus on not puking rather than reading. It doesn't even occur to me to be surprised or angry at my mom's response. This is normal. I'm too far away to be dealt with. My parents never pick me up now that my high school is located across town. I'm in too much pain to feel anything save the acceptance settling in my rib cage. This is the way it is. This is the way it will always be: Asking for help does no good. I'm the oldest of five kids, and the oldest must always make sacrifices.

Ten years later I find out most parents pick their kids up from school when they get migraines, even if it's the fourth one that month. When I hear this, the acceptance tangles into a knot. I'm fiercely proud of my independence, that I didn't *need* my parents. But I remember the way I hunched over my desk, trying to get through the day. My eyes try to fill with tears for my past self, but it was so common all I notice is an itch behind my eyelids. I've separated myself from emotion, because if I cry my head will hurt worse.

As I write these words, I feel the pain in my head acutely. It's in my temples, mainly my right. I still have a scab on my temple from an ice burn I accidentally gave myself a week ago.

It sounds like my parents are terrible. They really aren't. Let me say that again—they aren't.

You see, when you're a dramatic kid and have other family members who tend to be on the hypochondriac scale, saying you're in so much pain you want to claw your brains out isn't anything to write home about. Mental illness runs in my family, so my parents are extremely well-versed in dealing with it. As my dad said once, when you're dealing with mental illness, sure, it's invisible, but you deal with *more* of that person. Highs are extra high. Lows are extra low. You have that person *and more so.*

A chronic illness is a different type of invisible. You're not dealing with *more* of a person. You're dealing with *less.* My parents searched for signs of *more.* And were very good at spotting it. They just weren't as good at searching for signs of *less.* They don't notice when my personality fades or when the fear of pain creeps into existence. They don't notice the way I shrink from light and hide for a day in the dark.

I let my head rest fully on my desk again. Another day of moving my migrained-self from surface to surface until the bus can take me home. I'm an A student, so my teachers don't care if I check out for the day, and I'm too busy sleeping through the periods to see how my fellow students respond.

It's the last time I ask my parents to pick me up from school.

When I get home, I lay with my back facing the massive movie-worthy living room windows and hide my face in the cushions. The Bakersfield heat crawls down my back. Sweat drips through my bra and soaks the front of my shirt. My eyes are so heavy, it takes all my energy to focus them. Even my arms are dead weights, like heavy sawed-off logs attached to my body.

I don't have enough Imitrex to try to abort every attack. You take an abortive as soon as you have the earliest sign of migraine, which for me, is the aura. The Imitrex should halt the migraine from developing. This triptan class of abortives came out in the 90's and is currently the go-to *last-chance-to-stop-this-migraine-train* medication prescribed. They don't work well for me, and the Imitrex gives me the sensation of being drained of all my lifeblood.

My three youngest siblings' laughter drifts toward me. Peter Pan and the princesses chase each other in our basement. My dad waits outside for them dressed in an adult-sized Captain Hook outfit. Anna, my other sister, has a friend over upstairs, and their dance music drifts over the balcony. My mom cooks in the kitchen, roasting chicken for a salad.

Even though I can't participate, by lying in the living room I can still be a part of my family. I can still hear their chatter, still hear their stories. Even if my tongue weighs twenty pounds and I cannot tell my own.

They are all 3-D, but I'm stuck in 1-D, a tiny unnoticed dot. But pointillism shows us that enough dots can still tell their story.

5

I stand outside a garden. I'm in a good mood today, no migraines this week, so the breeze is light. I'm glad I'm not wearing anything heavier than jeans and a light crimson sweater. A white iron rod fence extends in front of me, stretching out of view into the draping trees. I try the gate, and it's unlocked. Somehow, I know it will always be unlocked for me. It's my garden, after all. It lives in my mind.

I got this idea in elementary school after scouring my grandmother's shelves for something interesting to read. Instead of a Nancy Drew book, I found a collection of prayers, all written during the author's time in a garden. The idea came to me: Why not try to meet God in a metaphysical garden? It felt far less stuffy than the routine prayers I was used to. So I created one in my mind with the intention of meeting Jesus there.

I push on the bars, and the gate swings open into lush green grasses and a myriad of trees. The scent of roses and honeysuckle is heady, but I breathe deeply and fill my lungs with the scent. It smells like stepping into beauty.

A paved pebble path appears and leads from the garden gate to a red-bricked building, where a wooden bench sits in front, inviting exhausted bones to rest. Even though it's my garden, I have not explored its depths, and I don't know what the building is yet. But I do know the bench looks inviting. I am nearing my high school graduation, and I am already tired.

I push away the branches of a weeping willow, stepping toward the bench. By the time I arrive, a man sits there. He wears mostly modern clothing, thick brown trousers and a white T-shirt. His hair is dark and curling near the back of the neck, echoing the swooping pattern of the iron fence. His skin is not white, but I can't pin the exact hue either. And His face—whenever I blink, I lose the specifics of His features. A predominant nose. Hazel eyes that border on green. I cannot tell if He has a beard. But whenever I try to draw this face, nothing but a blur greets me. As though my memory cannot hold onto this moment.

"I hoped you'd show up," I say.

I help myself to a seat next to Him. Though in real life I'm 5'10", here my feet can swing back and forth without touching the ground. Above me, glimpses of a fairy-tale sky break through the trees and birds playfully chirp. Picturesque is an understatement.

"I've been waiting for you," He says. His voice sounds

like sunshine caught on a rock by the river, like the breath between two golden music notes.

"How long have you been waiting?"

"I am always here."

And I know it's true. I have only one rule when I set up these surreptitious meetings: Write everything down. Even when I feel stupid. Despite the beauty of this place, anxiety rides my veins. "How am I supposed to do this? Put words into Your mouth when I know they are going on a page for everyone to read?"

Jesus watches the breeze caress the petals of a rose bush to our right. "I am still Me. I am the beginning, the end, and the middle. I Am constant."

"I will rewrite this scene a thousand times, won't I? Because I will always distrust myself, think I made a mistake, want to take it back . . ."

"And a thousand times I will be with you."

I nod, and we sit together in peace. Eventually, I hear my mother calling me to dinner. I can smell the acid notes of too many tomatoes in the goulash again. I'd rather stay here than choke down the miserable fruit. She calls my name again, harsher this time.

I slide off the bench. "You'll be here when I get back?"

"Abby, I am always here, waiting for you."

6

The first time I experience healing prayer is during my last semester in high school.

I am in a back room of my church on a Tuesday night, surrounded by the congregation's "prayer warriors," those who pray regularly on behalf of others. The carpet is old and peeling. The wood paneling is a light wooden hue. The air smells faintly of old people.

I don't know why I joined the group in the first place. My friend might've convinced me, or I was bored and needed something to do after soccer practice. But I love this back room. I love gathering with those older than me. These prayer meetings are like getting an inside view to the church, the innerworkings where everything happens as we pray over future sermons and the ebb and flow of the congregation at large. I love hearing the whispered requests and seeing the ways God says *yes*. Anything is possible. We sit in stackable chairs, all of them currently in a circle, facing each other.

I will go on to experience healing prayer in a myriad of ways. But they almost always start like this: Someone stands, says, "I feel a burden to pray for Abby and her migraines."

They've been getting worse. More and more frequent, more and more severe. Most of the time, when I arrive for the meeting, I am in some sort of pain.

A soft dread fills me. I don't mind being the center of attention. In fact, I love it, love the spotlight. But I've prayed countless times for the pain to stop, will pray a thousand more, and so far—nothing has happened. There's nothing in me that hints tonight will be the night, that tonight I'll walk away migraine-free. If anything, I hear a low-grade *no* building in my system.

"Oh, it's okay. I don't need—"

"No, really. We will pray for you."

There's the echo of, "Yes, Lord, please."

I don't doubt their sincerity. I don't doubt that God answers their prayers. I've seen it. I've heard it. I've participated in it. But shouldn't I know more than anyone if my life was going to change?

They stand as one and lay hands on me: dry palms, cracked palms, calloused palms, sweaty palms along the length of my arms. Another hand gently touches the back of my head, light as air. Another, my shoulder.

It won't work, I think. *It won't.* My friend gives me an encouraging smile from across the room. She has her hand linked through another's, who links through another's, and another's until the chain ends with yet another hand on my elbow.

Then the prayers start. At first, it's like music stuck in pianissimo, a quiet, gentle song. Gradually, it builds and builds, a crescendo, until twenty voices reach a melodious forte. I hear a mix of English and Spanish and something that doesn't sound quite human. Eventually, the music calms down and all those palms are removed.

"Well?" someone asks.

But the pain in my head from the previous migraine aura is still there, like an animal buried deep underground. "I'm sorry," I say.

Their faces are crestfallen. Hands pat my shoulders. I can't tell if I feel terrible because of the natural side effects of pain or because the prayer failed or because somehow they think *I* failed because I didn't have enough faith. I square my shoulders. If the latter, they're wrong. If the reason I walk away unhealed is because of a lack of faith on my part, that means I bear the responsibility of my healing. That it's my fault I'm sick. And I don't believe that to be true. If I walk away unhealed because God said no, then the responsibility and blame rests fully on His shoulders.

"Maybe next time," they say.

"Maybe," I say back.

I doubt it. The *no* is still thrumming in my core.

7

The aura starts by blurring out the road. The mountain pass is severe, with jagged rocks threatening to fall on either side. Avalanche nets keep any potential threat in place. There are only a couple ways to travel from Denver to Breckenridge, where I currently live on a national forest ranch to work during the summer leading into college. And they all include windy, twisting roads.

I accelerate.

My parents decide to have their midlife crisis early. But instead of having an affair or buying a too-expensive cherry-red car like the couple next door, they decide to go to seminary. A week ago, I found a voice message on my phone: "We're moving to Denver! Want to drive down and help us unpack?"

So I do. And on the way back, the migraine strikes.

It's a fast growing one. I'll be blind soon if I don't get to the ranch in time. I look to either side of the road. There are no pull-over spots. I grip the wheel harder and accelerate again.

I'm hitting 90, way too fast for these roads, but I manage to make it back before I'm completely blind. I stumble inside my refurbished tack house, nearly vomiting over the entry mat. I grope for the painkillers, as I've long since stopped taking Imitrex. Some mixture of Tylenol, Advil, and Excedrin. I swallow a handful and wait for the pain to slow.

It doesn't. The pain increases, a searing stabbing that cuts deep into my skull.

I take the next handful of pills. I lean against the coffee-colored sofa, head clutched in my hands and wait. The meds do nothing.

I take the next handful.

And the next.

And the next.

Until the world around me cartwheels and lines and edges start to blur. Tiredness creeps in, but it's not a natural tiredness. It's too forceful. Figures step out of the dark, like the echoes of ghosts. My throat clamps, and I scoot away from them. My heart rampages. *Make it stop, God, make it stop.* They reach knobby fingers at me, and my yell refuses to escape. I stumble toward the stairs, tripping over the first step, as the ghost-like figures continue to reach for me.

I'm hallucinating. That's what this is. Hallucinations.

I took too many pills.

But the realization doesn't make the figures fade.

I crawl into bed and shut my eyes. *What do I do? Who do I call?* I fumble for my phone and dial a friend. She doesn't answer. The tiredness is heavy now, dragging at my eyelids. I don't think to call an ambulance. Ambulances are for people who are dying from heart attacks or strokes or car crashes. They aren't for people like me. I curl up tight, head again clutched in my fingers.

I only have one thought: *God, please let me wake up.*

The darkness slips over me like a velvet blanket.

I eventually wake to sunlight on my cheeks. I slide my hands over my body to check that my parts haven't erased themselves during the night. To my surprise, everything is where it should be. I'm alive and in one piece. The wonder tastes candy sweet. Until I move my head—

The pain is still there.

8

Growing up, I wanted to be a paleontologist. I spent hours poring over books, memorizing all the different dino names so I could impress my friends with my shiny eighteen letter words. You know, casually drop them in a conversation with all an eight-year-old's skill. When I ran out of dinosaur books, I discovered missionaries and explorers. I really only had access to books about missionaries, because I mostly raided my parent's bookshelves, so I read and reread those. Regardless of my mixed feelings about missionaries and explorers now, the stories of those who traveled to the unknown and discovered new lands and people and languages fueled my imagination.

Then I discovered archeologists. I don't know if it was Indiana Jones or my mother's *Walk through the Bible* video series I came home to on weekdays, but something in me clicked. I could travel! I could study history! I could be chased through the desert in a grungy red jeep while being shot at by bad guys! Don't get me started on the moment I discovered *Lara Croft: Tomb Raider*.

A biblical archeologist came to speak at our church, claiming to have discovered the real Mount Sinai. I devoured his books, storing all those facts or pseudo-facts. I borrowed the crap out of my church library, which mainly held Amish romance novels and various postapocalyptic novels set in Israel. (Guess which of the two I went for?)

I spent several years gathering as much historical data as I could manage. I even studied the Old Testament *for fun*—until I actually met an archeologist who wasn't trying to market a recently released book. Apparently, seventy-five percent of archeology is paperwork. Twenty-five percent is field work. Zero percent is being chased through the desert in a grungy red jeep while being shot by bad guys.

I promptly switched my life goal.

Enter my astronomy and astronaut phase. This lasted until I took freshman high school biology and realized I'd have to take more science classes like this to see the stars. (Ten years too late, I understand there's a difference between biology and physics.)

After the stars comes photojournalism, thanks to binge reading all the Tintin comics once a year while visiting my dad's side of the family. Then I took photography in high school and dabbled in regular journalism, with the intention of heading overseas to die in a political uprising while delivering the truth. Thanks, Marie Colvin and Nellie Bly.

Eventually I settled for working in a church. It was not the most exciting career I could come up with, but I figured I could make it into an adventure. My family is deeply religious and loves Jesus and tries to follow his teachings with every aspect of their lives. I lived my childhood life according to the rhythms and community of church events. Why not continue this into the future? Help run a church and somehow tie it into in journalism.

The hero's journey is never part of the plan, either. The hero has her own dream, her own picture for her future, her own ideal life. Enter the plot twist and the call to action. The hero is swung away from her expected life onto an entirely new journey.

Remembering this makes bearing the pain easier.

The original plan was never intended to include pain. A plot twist, and now it's part of my new journey.

9

Second week of college, freshman year.

The wet heat in Chicago is a different sort of heat than the dry desert kind I grew up with. Even in the suburbs, the thick, damp humidity drifting from the lake clings to the air like a wet sock. My first purchase for my dorm isn't cute curtains, but a rotating fan. My roommate, Kelly, and I take turns standing in front of the blades, airing out our armpits.

For those first two weeks, I'm Hermione embodied, and not just because of what humidity does to my hair. Excitement thrums through me as I dress for class every day. I *want* to do homework because it feels more important than high school homework. Like this assignment is something that would actually contribute to my life. For an extrovert who lived forty-five minutes away from her high school, living with *forty-nine* other girls *right outside her door* is nothing short of a fairy-tale.

The only thing I remember from the first half of the

semester is my gen-ed health class. It's one of those classes where you're supposed to catalogue your exercise, but there's no real way for the prof to know whether or not you played Settlers the whole time instead. The class is filled with a healthy mix of class years, and everybody is a possible future best friend. Which turns out to be true.

My future best friend is in the class. If I'd known we'd be in each other's lives for as long as we have been, I would've jumped over all the tables and dragged her chair over to mine.

I wish this Tuesday is special. I wish I have some foreboding sensation or see a blood red comet streaking across the sky. I wish something, *anything* spectacular happens to set apart this day from all the rest. But the truth is, it's your normal, average Tuesday. I eat eggs for breakfast, wear mom jeans that aren't cool yet because I still don't know how to pick out a flattering pair of pants; and, since I'll be working out later, probably haven't even showered.

The class runs long, and this hour is one of the first times since I walked onto campus that I actually have to sit still and be in my body. In the quiet and droning lecture, I notice something.

Throb. Throb. Throb.

I close my eyes and press my fingers to my temple. Right —there. My veins pulse with the rhythm.

Throb. Throb. Throb.

The pain is almost as bad as a migraine, but there's no aura and it's not quite as sharp. Sure, the migraines have been getting worse. I've gone from getting several a month to a couple a week, and I started developing hours and hours of auras at a time, but pain without an aura is new.

Throb. Throb. Throb.

It's definitely cutting in on my daydreaming.

I tap the shoulder of the tall blonde next to me. "Do you have Advil?" I whisper.

"No, but I got Excedrin." She digs in her backpack. Carrying a backpack as a college student is way cooler than using one in high school. As though you're too brilliant and need extra support to carry around all your smarts.

The pills taste like chalk and take their time moseying down my throat. They don't really help, but it takes the edge off enough so I can sort-of focus on the prof. Better than Advil, at least.

The next time I'm in the gen-ed class, the *throb throb throb* is back.

I nudge my neighbor again. "Hey, sorry. Do you have any more Excedrin?"

Another dig through the backpack. Another dry swallow.

I bring Excedrin the next week. I realize: Every time I'm in this class, my head throbs. I'm so good at compartmentalizing, it takes me another week to realize: Hey, it's not only during this gen-ed health class. The throbbing permeates, not just other hours, but almost every day.

It's bad enough for me to need medicine. Bad enough for the medicine not to help. Bad enough to send me to the nurses' station, where I explain to the on-campus doctor that, "It can't be a caffeine headache. The throbbing started *before*

I took Excedrin." Bad enough for them to shrug and suggest seeing a specialist. Bad enough that it interferes with my thinking, like a softer migraine, except there's still no aura anywhere.

So what the hell is this?

10

I meet my husband because of a migraine.

Well. Technically, I already met Randy on the first day of college, because he and his roommates decide to be gentlemen and introduce themselves to all the freshmen girls. In case anybody had questions or needed help finishing moving in. A true act of altruism.

But we become *friends* because of a migraine.

It's the first Saturday of my college career. I spend the entire day in my dorm with your friendly neighborhood aura and nothing but Kelly's good graces for company. The antsiness crawls along my bones, and I need *out*. At this point, I'm still fairly physically active, so if I spend a whole day in bed, restlessness gnaws.

Most weekend nights, the dorm has something called "open floor," where the girls and guys enter each other's floors and hang during the evening. It's a normal procedure for a Christian college. This Saturday is not an open floor night, which means everybody's hanging *out*, not *in*. Besides, nobody wants to be *in* during the first real weekend of the school year.

I pull on a clean T-shirt and jeans and drag myself to the common area just so I can spot another human being that isn't my roommate.

I settle in one of the indestructible chairs, content to sit in the brain fog and hazy pain and to watch others have fun. Students burst in and out of the halls, running up and down the stairs, to and from events, giving me a glimpse of what I could've been doing if not for this stupid migraine.

I recognize Randy from earlier in the week. He mans the stairwell door for others, checking his phone, opening the door again, checking his phone. His bright red shirt draws out the tones in his tanned skin. His phone dings again. He opens the door, and I realize what he's actually doing—debating about leaving the room.

I finally speak up. "You're Randy, right? A sophomore?"

"Yeah! Good memory." He hasn't looked away from his phone. "You planning on people watching all night?"

"Most likely," I say. "I'm not feeling too great. Do you need to go somewhere?"

A group of girls wearing short dresses and a generous amount of hair spray stride past, giggling at him. He still doesn't look up. "I'm actually trying to decide if I can*not* go somewhere."

I raise an eyebrow, but not at the half-dressed boy scootering along the hallway. "I so badly want to go somewhere I dragged myself out here. Where do you not want to go?"

He gives an exaggerated sigh. "It's a long story. Short version: I've got a group of friends who want to watch a movie tonight. Except, I've been trying to get out of the group. I just feel bad about it."

"So you're looking for an excuse."

"Pretty much." He finally fully looks at me. His eyes are a kind brown, the type that makes you instantly think of melted chocolate. "Hey. You said you don't feel good?"

"Yeah. Migraine."

"That sucks. It hurts?"

Like a bitch. "Yep."

"You'll need company, then. Right?"

There isn't anybody else around now save scooter-boy. I'd already met a ton of stupid guys this week, but Randy doesn't seem like one of them. And those bulges along his sleeve whisper of muscles. I like a good set of muscles. And his grinning cheeks are punctured by these deep dimples you can bury your thumb into. I like dimples. And I really, *really* like dark-haired men.

"Sure."

Maybe this night isn't going to be so bad after all.

"Cool." He types out a quick text. "I'm telling them I can't come because my friend needs some help."

"We're friends?"

"Now we are." He shoves his phone in his pocket and slides into the seat next to me. He's all smiles and defined forearms-on-knees and ready-to-go conversation. "What's your name again?"

11

My family chooses to spend the holidays at my grandparents' place along the central California coast. Reading only makes the migraine pain worse, so I spend hours diddling in my grandma's art room since there isn't much else to do save walk in the drizzly fog. The walls are plastered with watercolor paintings, and my grandma offers me an unsuccessful watercolor lesson. My brush refuses to create even the simplest stroke. I switch to pencils. I find a cute photo I took in high school of a kid wearing a construction hat. Each attempt at the portrait looks no better than my eight-year-old sister's scribbles. After several hours of meandering lines, I give up entirely.

That night I have a dream.

In my dream, I paint a giraffe's eye and watch the colors smear together. I paint over and over again, brush stroke after brush stroke, until my brain clicks and something unlocks. I can't explain it, besides chalking the experience up to a divine art lesson. The next morning, I try the portrait again. My hands suddenly know what to do. They smear the graphite across the page, creating dimension and—surprise! —a lifelike face.

My insides break open. I draw portraits again, again, again, practicing the technique I saw in my dream. The drawings aren't amazing by any stretch. Nothing to hang in a museum. But the vast difference between my scrambled-egg lines the day before and a face I can recognize . . . I appear almost talented. For the rest of the break, pain doesn't matter. I'm stuck in wonder that my hands can create meaning beyond their true capability.

12

"You want me to go with you, Abby?" Kelly watches me cram my backpack full of books to study in the waiting room. She's wearing volleyball shorts and stretches out her hamstrings on our Christmas-hued second-hand couch while sipping from an Arnold Palmer. The shelves above her desk are a shrine to how much she loves the drink. Neither of us bothers to decorate our dorm, not because we don't want to, but because it doesn't occur to us. "I can skip practice," she says. "My coach will understand."

Autumn is right around the corner, my first real autumn with foliage more colorful than a palm tree. Our fan spins only half the day now, and we no longer take turns drying the sweat off our bodies. In a couple weeks, I'll be eighteen.

I double-check my wallet, making sure I have my insurance card. Then double-check my planner to make sure I'm not missing any possible schoolwork. Filling my backpack gives my fingers something to do besides tap out an anxious beat against my leg. The anxiety will disappear as soon as I dive into reading in the waiting room.

I'm ready to go. "No," I say. "I'll be fine."

This is true. I will be fine. I'm always fine. The idea of saying, *Yes, come*, never occurs to me, because that's what a migraine means: dealing with the consequences myself. Like being stuck at school. Or that awful night in the tack house. Nobody will save me except myself.

I regret not taking her with me as soon as I step inside the hospital. Hospitals are meant to fix you, not make you comfortable. They want you to check in, get fixed, then they want you out. I've always wondered if somebody *not sick* designed the space. As if they were afraid a comfortable hospital meant patients would want to stay.

"Sign here." The secretary points to a line on the form. "Have you ever done an echocardiogram before?"

I readjust my backpack and scribble my signature on the line. "Nope."

"It will be fine. I'm sure of it." She gives me a weak smile and gestures toward the open seating. "You'll be going back soon."

Half an hour passes while I tap my toes against the floor. The walls are a seasick green, and when I stare at the ceiling, little intrusive faces appear in the popcorn pattern. I try to knock out some homework, but I can't get more than a couple chapters into my assigned reading. I wasn't expecting to be this nervous. The anxiety doesn't disappear, but creeps through my body—slow and sluggish and stinging.

Thankfully I'm not claustrophobic, because the inside of

a CT scanner is a bit white and tight. Or at least, it should be white . . . *Whomp whomp whomp whomp*. The noise sounds like a localized earthquake, shaking only my eardrums.

I squint and twist to see the gray spot better. That spot around 10 o'clock isn't gray at all. In fact, it's . . .

My gut sinks faster than a free-falling lift. The spot flashes multi-colored. This is an aura. And I'm stuck inside a space-tube for the next God-knows-how-long. Without medicine. Which is about twenty feet away in my purse.

Whomp whomp whomp whomp.

"Try not to move," the voice over the intercom says.

I quit wriggling. I try to ignore the spot twisting, turning, growing, spreading across my vision. The pain blossoms across my skull.

After a couple minutes, the nurse slides me out like a corpse in the morgue. Thank God. Thank God. I can still get my meds—

"Did he want contrast?" the nurse says.

"Uh." *What the hell's* contrast? *I'm not done?* "I dunno, but can—"

"Hold up, sweetie, lemme ask." She turns toward the man in the window. The way he sits reminds me of a cop in a detective show behind the interrogation window. "Hey, Bill. BIIIIiiilll. Yeah, you. Did the doc ask for contrast?"

A nod.

"Okay, sweetie. Gimme a sec."

The needle pricks my vein on the second try. The IV fluid burns like fire-ice in my blood, strong enough to distract me from the throbbing pain in my head. The nurse slides me back into the morgue-machine with the same flourish right before a cut-scene.

No clues found here, detective.

Whomp whomp whomp whomp.

This is the first interrogation of my brain. Maybe we could get Miss Brain to talk. What secrets are you hiding? What clues lay below the surface?

By the time I finish, the migraine is at its zenith, and my legs are jelly. I jab my hand into my purse and fumble for the narcotics. My current doctor agrees I needed stronger medication instead of trying to mix and match a variety of mediocre meds to make a dent in the pain.

We stop to talk to Bill on the way back to the waiting room.

"Wanna see the photos?" He speaks with all the enthusiasm of someone who truly enjoys their job.

"Dear heavens, yes," I say. What does a migraine look like on screen? Can you see the neurological movement as the aura passed? What about at the end, when there's nothing but pure pain? What's going on inside my brain right now?

Bill jabs his finger across the multi-colored image. "You can see there's no unusual activity here—"

No unusual activity?

I spent the last how many minutes with an aura, and there's no unusual activity?

Csssshhhht. A pop of a microphone. *Sorry, sir, the suspect has not entered the building. No unusual activity here. Must've read the clues wrong.*

"—And this is the version with contrast and . . . Er." His finger pauses above a dark spot on the screen. He glances, desperate, at the nurse beside me. Clearly, something's not supposed to be there. He not-so-subtly nudges the nurse, who hustles me out of sight of the screens.

The interrogation's over. We'd finally gotten the truth from my brain. The dark spot proves it.

I spend the next week with my phone in my pocket, ready to answer, dreaming about what life could be like after we fix the dark spot. A tumor. It has to be a tumor. Take a tumor out, skip a little school, get a little sympathy from current crush Randy, move on with my life.

Ring ring. Please come into the doctor's office, we have something important to talk to you about.

But the phone call never comes.

A month later, *I* phone my doctor for a follow-up. Soon as I walk in, I spot the folder with my name printed on the tab. The folder with images from the CT scan with the dark spot. The folder that holds my brain's secrets. We spend two-thirds of the appointment chatting about my current treatment plan, how it isn't working, how the narcotics are helpful for the aura migraines but the daily pain is still there, yada yada yada.

Then he finally, finally, finally, reaches for the folder and draws out the photo.

My heart rate accelerates. This is it! THIS IS IT.

"So your CT scan shows you're clean."

"Clean?" I blink. *How can it be clean?* I practically grab the image from his hand. "So there's . . . nothing?"

Subtext: no aura, no migraine, nothing to show for this pain?

"Well." He points to the dark spot. "You do have this minor benign cyst, but where it's located, it's not causing any pressure on your brain, not invading anything. It's just . . . There."

"Harmless?"

"Completely. They're very common. You'll take another scan in a year, just to double-check it didn't grow. But I'm very certain it won't."

I look at the CT scan. No unusual activity.

Here's where some of the many guilt complexes slide in. You *want* a bad diagnosis. A bad diagnosis means something can be fixed. You feel so hypocritical and guilty because you *want* the doctor to hold your hand and wipe your tears after they drop the "tumor" or "cancer" bomb. Because tumor and cancer is an answer, and you're no longer left standing in the mystery. Because nothing is worse than pain without a *why.*

Then you add another layer of guilt, because there are many people with tumors and cancer who'd trade all your pain in a *wagooshing* heartbeat. If I'm truly being honest, sometimes, especially on my bad days, I wish I *could* make the trade.

Add another layer of guilt.

"So," I say. "What's next?"

The doc bites his lower lip. "Unfortunately, I don't know what else to do for you. I've run through all my options, all my tests. I can't help you. I'm sorry."

We can't hold you without probable cause. You're dismissed.

I walk into the empty waiting room filled with strangers. Why am I surprised? Of course Kelly isn't there. I didn't want her for the initial scan. I didn't want her for this follow-up. I wish now I had brought her. Just so I could see a familiar face and tell someone, *No news is bad news*. Just so I can have somebody, anybody, to hold my hand and let me cry.

It's the first time I realize: My body isn't playing for the same team I am.

13

Chicago's spring is filled with crimson tulips and whistling icy wind. It knifes though me, and I pull my trench coat in closer. I know the sun will shine again and students will be basking on the green lawns to soak the rays, but it's hard to believe when there's been nothing but a velvet gray sky for the last month.

Classes will be done in several weeks, and I will have survived my first year of college. But right now, each step toward the cafeteria sends a punch to my temples. My numb fingers fumble for my cell. I scroll through my contacts until I find my home phone number and call.

My youngest sister's childlike voice is the recording for the answering machine. *You've reached the Shane Gang. Leave a message!* My family is notorious for not answering the phone, so there's most likely someone lurking around.

I try again.

This time, my mom answers.

In the background, my youngest siblings squabble, and I hear Anna's voice trying to boss them into line.

"Watcha need? I'm in the middle of cooking dinner." My mom doesn't mean to be curt. She just has four other children at home, a husband struggling with severe depression, and a to-do list a mile long. Instead of buying a shiny apple-red convertible when their mid-life crisis hit, both my parents decided to return to grad school. And that included homework, papers, and assigned reading.

"I just wanted to say hi." What I don't say: *My head hurts again, and I just want to hear your voice and know everything is going to be okay.*

"You've been calling every day for the last two weeks."

"I know."

"You shouldn't be calling here so often. You should be with your friends."

My stomach free falls into my kitten heels. I pull back to stare at the screen. Did she really just say what I think she said? I can still hear my siblings fighting in the background. I imagine her slicing potatoes for a roast with the phone pinned to her face by her shoulder, thoughts more on calling the dentist to reschedule an appointment than on me.

She wants me to stop calling.

I can't help you. Nobody can help you through this pain.

It's like being in high school all over again. Parents can't help me. Teachers can't help me. Better to lay my head on a desk and wait for the pain to run its course. If the pain ever does.

I make up some excuse to hang up.
I don't call home again for a very long time.

14

Randy is the type of guy you notice.

Not because he's tall. (He's not. I've got two inches on him). Not because he's the most handsome guy in the room (though I'm biased). Not because his charismatic energy draws you in like a magnet (I mean, he pulled me into his orbit). But because, when you enter a conversation with him, he hyper-focuses on you so that for a time you are the only thing in his universe. You come away knowing you were truly, deeply seen.

It's my junior year, and he stands in the doorway of my on-campus apartment holding a sandwich and cookie, again wearing my favorite shade of red. I am too migraine-y to get food for myself, so he brings it to me. He lays beside me while I try to stave off the dizziness by staring at the darkened cheap ceiling light. He doesn't talk about his dreams of being a pastor, of impacting people on a personal level. He only lays beside me and breaks off the crusts before handing the PB&J over piece by piece.

He takes my hand and gently rubs his giant thumb over my knuckles, humming a song I can cling to through the pain.

He's the first person to ever sit with me through a migraine.

I didn't plan on getting married young, certainly not as young as twenty, but when Randy first broaches the subject, I grow curious to see what life would look like with this particular adventure. I love him. I love the way he encourages me. I love the way he pushes me into unknown territory. I love the way he pursues my emotions, even when I don't want to acknowledge them. I love how he embodies love.

When he gets down on one knee during our one-year dating anniversary in the middle of a pine grove, I say yes.

15

My engagement ring is still sparkly with newness when my phone buzzes with a text message from a friend. He asks if I have any recommendations of places to visit during his trip to Israel. I've never been more grateful to be Type A. Every map, book, note, including a field diary, is tucked neatly into my personal journal.

I snap photos of everything and text them along, then spend an hour sinking into my journal and memories. I had the privilege to travel to both Israel and England during summer study abroad programs, which allowed me to graduate an entire year early. I knew my migraines were a kind-of-sort-of-a-problem (if there's no body, did a crime even occur?) and wasn't sure if travel would be possible, so I spoke with the professors in charge to figure out if I could even do the programs.

When I look back on the trips, I remember one aura migraine.

My journal contradicts this. I didn't have one aura, but many, on top of the daily pain. Even though I didn't bother spending time scribbling about the pain every time I wrote, the pain impacted how people saw me.

A friend pulled me aside during a hot hike up Masada. "You're such an encouragement."

"I admire how you trust God through the pain."

"*Inspirational.*"

The words were an encouragement to me. I wasn't aware I was doing anything special. I was just being me.

It's the first time I see how my memory doesn't match up to reality. There's a disconnect between what I think happened and what really happened.

My memory also tells me I'd only considered writing during my final semester of college. Even then, I swear I never thought about writing fiction.

My journal says otherwise.

I started dreaming about being a writer, about crafting my own adventures, as early as junior high. Halfway through my sophomore year in high school, I'd begun wondering if I had "the soul of a novelist." Which is such a romantic turn of phrase it belongs in a cheap rom-com. I find brainstorming lists of different ways to use writing in my life. I unearth notes about small writing internships I completed for other authors and creators I'd completely forgotten about.

In my memory, I decide to write because I can do nothing else. Reality says writing has always been a part of me. I was already dreaming of pursuing this career. "I have decided I am going to be published," I wrote in the eighth grade. In my journals I wrote about the way words feel, how stories glow in my chest.

I'm never happier than when I'm writing a story.

There were two literature professors I admired in college: Lundin and Foster. Both died a handful of years ago within weeks of each other. I was never the type of student who sought out their professors. I wish I was. But I was always too embarrassed. I wasn't one of the "star pupils," and I assumed only "star pupils" have great relationships with their professors. I missed classes and wore a zombie glaze due to pain in the ones I did attend, when I wasn't dashing out due to narcotic nausea.

When I am a handful of months from both graduation and marrying, I figure if I am brave enough to say lifelong vows, then I better be brave enough to schedule a social call with my professors. I meet with Foster first, and we talk about sonnets and structure and boundaries and how living within limits can actually provide the most freedom. A twist on what Madeleine L'Engle once said: "Life with its rules, its obligations, and its freedoms, is like a sonnet: You're given the form, but you have to write the sonnet yourself."

Living within my limits like a sonnet. What a strange idea.

Lundin and I talk about the metaphysical relationship between objects and symbols (you know, since everybody talks about these things in college). He sips from his mug. "Do you have any plans for after graduating? Or any plans on how you want to use your English degree?" He's tall and lean and has the type of smile that makes you want to be enthusiastically truthful.

I lean back in my chair. "I want to be a writer."

Lundin blinks at me for a moment. He gets all the credit for taking me seriously. Then we talk about my grades. I didn't receive the best grades, not because my logic isn't sound, but because I can never find the right words I need to express myself.

"You know what might help you?" he says.

"I should read more?"

"Yes, but find some writers you admire and study how they use words. Get to know their language backward and forward. That will help."

Now I know he meant *voice.*

He's trying to tell me, gently, that I have no voice.

I remember internalizing his critique as: I am the kid who wants to be a writer but doesn't know how to use words.

My journal says otherwise.

I scribble furiously back in my apartment: "I might not know the right words now, but I can learn them. And besides, isn't most of writing about grit and determination? Well, I've got enough grit for two people. I should be just fine."

16

As a capstone assignment for my senior English portfolio, we're supposed to do something, *anything*, for thirty days. We will write every day and then, at the end of the period, turn it into a magical work of nonfiction. One of the other girls doesn't wear makeup for an entire month. Inner beauty or something like that. I tried not wearing makeup for Lent once, and it happened to be the biggest breakout of my life. Not doing that again.

There's really only one rule to the assignment: No matter what happens, you write it down, because you might find a story in your ramblings.

At the time, I attend school-wide chapels three times a week. If you're not familiar with chapels, they consist of about forty-five mandatory minutes of community and worship. Half the students hate it. I enjoy the variety. Musicians, speakers, sermons, ministries—all have their time to shine. In some of my favorite chapels, we use liturgy.

Although church was the rhythm of my life, I was not steeped in the historical traditions of the church. I was proud that I didn't practice things like Lent or Advent. Tradition was shackles, and I, the rebel who tread my own path. Like most "nondenominationals" (which meant I was not tied to a particular Christian sub movement), I had no clue what liturgy is. Why would I use somebody else's words when I can ask God whatever I want? Why does it matter?

Growing up, the closest I got to a liturgy was communion once a month, the tiny wafers and sip of faux-wine I treated like an anorexic mid-morning snack. Now, I discover liturgy is not simply preprogrammed sentences designed to bore you into compliance. There's more to it. Liturgy is prayers people have been saying for hundreds of years. Saying these is like stepping into a living history book. Though the words are old, they are something new. And for someone who largely grew up without structure to guide my faith, reading something preprogrammed is interesting.

Why not learn more?

So I commit to praying liturgy for my thirty-day writing project.

A quick Amazon search gives me a cheap *Book of Prayer*, which lays out phrases, prayers, and verses for four times a day, for an entire thirty days. I set my alarm and start.

And I fall in love.

Four times a day, time melds into one. Four times a day, I repeat the past, and the past becomes the now. Four times a day, I live history. Four times a day, I write whatever I'm thinking.

Easy enough.

At the end of the experiment, I have a couple weeks to compile all my ramblings into a story. I sit to read my wondrous, amazing thoughts that will most definitely get me an A (finally) and prove Professor Lundin wrong. I flip through the pages of my notes to find—

Nothing brilliant.

No insights.

No amazing look into my inner soul.

Instead, I find four times a day, thirty days of pain.

I can barely get through the liturgy, can barely focus on the words, because of the pain in my head.

It throbbed. It hummed. It blurred the words. It stole my thoughts.

So I wrote that in my notebook. Four times a day, for thirty days, I had catalogued pain. All the ways it hurt. All the ways it took over my life.

This can't be right. Flip flip flip through pages. *My life doesn't feel like this. My life can't look like this.*

But there's the proof, in front of me. "My brain feels full of blood." *Oh yeah, I vaguely remember thinking that. Oh, this was an aura day, wasn't it? No? Just a normal day?*

My brain still feels full of blood.

AURA

The aura is the first visual and/or physical disturbance of a migraine in process. An aura can take the form of a numbing tingle crawling from your arm to your tongue or a C shape flickering that devours your vision. It starts suddenly, seemingly out of nowhere. It's a true Alice in Wonderland experience and what I imagine an acid trip would be like.

After simmering in the subconscious, an idea bursts into conscious thought in an explosion of rainbows and light and joy—a true out-of-body experience. The idea seemingly explodes from the darkness, ready to be worked with. The Muse touches you, and you are given a creative grace.

Genesis 1:3a
"Then God said, 'Let there be light . . .'"

17

After Randy and I graduate and marry, we move to Denver. There's a popular Christian nonfiction author, Sarah, who lives about twenty minutes away from our two-bedroom apartment. Through a random connection (the dentist of all places), Sarah emails asking if I'd be interested in possibly working for her with my shiny new English degree. I audition by writing some articles, and she hires me to join her staff to complete smaller writing tasks like blog posts and admin work so she can focus on writing her books and speaking.

I love kissing new-husband Randy in the mornings before I leave for work. I love having a coworker/office manager to talk to in the silent moments. I love my desk, which overlooks a majestic view of the Rocky Mountain foothills. No joke: deer peek inside a couple times a month. One pees right by my window. I love Sarah's energy and her husband's stories, and I'm happy.

I especially love reading over Sarah's work.

If anybody has *voice*, Sarah has it. Her words bubble off the page, and her sentences roll joyfully, just as she comes across in real life. In studying her work, I slowly understand what Lundin meant. When I come home, I type my own words, my first novel, while I cook dinner. Working part-time for Sarah is the best thing that could happen for my writing. It's a master-level inside look into the world of publishing. I also get really good at applying stamps to her thank-you letters and become friends with the post-office workers.

Except.

Pain.

Sarah leaves me part of her newest manuscript to read through. The pages are stacked in the corner of my desk. I can't focus on the words. I run my fingers along the pages. About twenty sheets left before I leave. This should be easy. I've even moved from my beloved desk so I can face a wall with significantly less light.

But I can't think past the pounding in my temples. I can't move without it reverberating along the rest of my skull.

I imagine scooping out my brain, rolling it out until it's as thin as a crepe. And c-u-t out the pain. I crumble the mass of infected flesh and shove it aside. *This pain no longer exists. I don't feel this.* I stuff the remainder of my brain back into my skull and focus.

This time when I come home, I cry.

The brain fog creeps into my other tasks. What should take fifteen minutes takes me an entire hour. The mental connection I should make in seconds takes several minutes. I can tell Sarah is growing frustrated, and rightly so, but I don't know what to do. The more I push through the pain, the more it pushes back. And the harder it pushes, the more I rely on my core strengths. Story is deeply built into my heart, and I can follow plot lines and character arcs even during the worst pain. But I'm not hired to create stories. I'm hired to do admin work.

I work part-time for Sarah for a year and a half before Randy insists on an appointment with my new neurologist.

Dr. Path is a small woman. I think my left thigh is as big as her. But her presence fills the room like a storm cloud, all at once and heavy. She sits across from me with my thick file and reads through her previous notes. I'm about to leave when an elbow jab in the ribs from Randy reminds me to ask the question. He has been attending my appointments as I underplay my symptoms, and he no longer believes I can accurately represent myself.

I wet my lips and say the words: "Is there anything else I can be doing besides taking new medication? I keep coming home from work in a lot of pain."

Dr. Path looks up from her notes, and, cross-my-heart, her eyes flash like lightning. "Yes. The best thing you can do is completely overhaul your lifestyle. Quit pushing your boundaries. Learn to live within them. Stop doing an activity if it causes pain."

I stare at her small form as my gut tightens into a knot and her words rattle around my skull like a marble in an empty can.

Stop doing an activity if it causes pain? What does that

even mean? There's always pain. *Learn to live within boundaries?* What does that even look like? The only visual I can come up with are the rules of a sonnet, again.

The ride home is quiet. Randy is in the driver's seat, quiet, lips so twisted from thinking that his dimples pop. Dr. Path's words sink deeper and deeper into both of us.

He breaks the silence. "You need to quit."

I don't look at him but at the fall leaves brushing past the car window. "Quit what?"

Don't say it. Please don't say it.

"Quit working for Sarah."

I'm not a quitter. I'm not.

But I can't keep living like this.

My gut releases as Randy's permission seeps in. *I don't* have *to keep living like this.* I can stop. The pain can stop.

It's one of the reasons I married him. He gives me permission to go where I'm afraid to go.

After tearful conversations and financial gymnastics, I quit, because the days I come home and cry from pain are now more frequent than the days I don't, and I can't deliver what Sarah wants.

The first morning I don't leave for work when I normally would have, the relief—and the guilt from the privilege of relief—is a tidal wave. It beats against my body, matching rhythm with my pounding head. Randy tucks a blanket around me on the couch, brings me an ice pack and the TV remote. He pulls out crayons and sets them on the table within reach. He whispers a prayer and gives me a kiss. "You did the right thing. You need this. You don't know how much you need this." Then he leaves for classes and work.

I'm in so much pain, I can't even see the great yawning space that is now my future. TV. Ice packs. Audiobooks. Darkness. I'm left in the silence, save for the still-stabbing, never-ending beat in my head.

18

If we are the hero of our own stories, then there's also a good chance we are the villain in somebody else's. Somewhere between playing My Little Pony and Nancy Drew computer games, I become one of Anna's villains.

Anna is the sister closest to me in age. She's two years younger, and I have almost six inches on her. She loves drama, delicate china teacups, white picket fences, and romance, and has already mapped out her entire future. When she steps into the sun, her hair glistens like crushed rubies.

It starts slowly. A missed conversation here. A harsh word there. The gap of age driving a wedge while my friends deal with the ethics of smoking and hers still play with American Girl dolls. And then the atmosphere shifts. My migraines cause mood swings before every aura. I grow more irritable, irrationally angry, and an ignored request to shut the door is reason enough for me to go to battle. Anna grows cold and moody, sharper in tongue, wanting an emotional bond I don't know how to give, and a misstep on prom night leads to a full-on meltdown.

Gone are the days when we used to play "Otter and Squirrel" in the pool. We circle around each other, complete opposites, waiting for the next move of our opponent.

Then, in college, I soften. Heart friends teach me how to engage emotionally. Randy teaches me how to remove my walls and invite someone in. I return home from college, ready to make full amends and step back into relationship.

Anna is not.

Her moods grow more and more irrational. Every word out of my mouth, however well intentioned, is taken the wrong way. I become one of the whipping boys for her anger. I write her off as "the sister who hates me for some reason" and "we're just too different to have a real relationship."

And then a phrase is reintroduced into our lives: Bipolar disorder.

It explains everything, from her moods to how she sees the world, to the inability to get out of bed one day, to the next morning's sudden desire to book a last-minute ticket to Paris.

She's been suffering in her own, invisible way.

How much of our relationship has been influenced by illness? If I were to guess, I'd say *a lot*. Maybe we'd have been best friends longer if neither of us were sick. Maybe our lives would've looked exactly the same.

All I know is that when she's forced to drop out of college for a while to deal with her mental illness, I decide to try to be supportive.

19

After I quit working, I quickly grow bored. My parents gift me lessons to a nearby watercolor studio as a Christmas present, and I quickly discover I have a knack for it. I begin to steep myself in art. I ravage the local library and YouTube my way to heaven. I study paintings and how-to books to figure out techniques. I also read blogposts about writing conferences to find summaries of workshops; I mine information from these summaries. I write in fifteen-minute chunks on a novel, with the computer screen turned off so that it doesn't aggravate the pain. When I can, I read and catalogue characters and techniques and stories.

I have another dream in the thick of this learning. In it, God and I walk along wooden hallways, studying art pieces and discussing them. We study a sculpture. It's the same horrid poop brown as my father-in-law's car; it's lumpy, and the proportions are off.

"How would you fix this?" God asks.

I stare at the mess until I see a solution. "Like this." I flip the sculpture upside down.

I start using this technique on my art. Whenever I get stuck on a watercolor piece, I literally flip it sideways, turn it upside down, until I can either see what's truly wrong or find a new solution. New perspectives lend objectivity. I don't realize this is an actual painting technique until a handful of years later.

Practicing new perspectives in my painting teaches my brain the flexibility to solve problems in writing.

How can I twist this story upside down? What do I need to flip over? How can I think outside the box for solutions? What if I were to literally turn this around? Cut sections here—move them there. Swap character arcs, twist them. I'm rarely afraid to cut sections or plot lines, to reframe facts to fit a new out-of-the-box solution. I can stand back and see objectively better because I've been practicing objectivity in another medium.

This ability to transfer a way of thinking from one medium to another is what I call "creative cross-training." Like an athlete cross-training in another sport to better their own, we can do the same with creative mediums.

Perhaps I would've eventually learned to problem-solve like this in writing. But I'm able to implement it much faster because I've been practicing with different media.

20

I stand at the bottom of the staircase leading to our apartment. I'm twenty-two, and it's been a whopping three months since I quit working. Inside my apartment is a stack of watercolor paintings, a mostly finished novel on my laptop, and an ice pack. I'm most looking forward to the ice pack.

A plastic sack of groceries hangs from my hands. Mini knives press against my skull. The stairs might as well be a mountain for how impossible they seem. I used all my energy grocery shopping and can't finish coming home.

My eyes sting. A blossoming ache spreads across my breastbone. I grip my groceries tight to keep from flinging them against the wall. To keep from *punching* the wall. Instead, I mentally beat the brick over and over until my knuckles bleed. Because if I did it in real life, the action would only make the pain worse.

Like everything else.

Did Dr. Path know that showering, that standing up, that the motion of making a sandwich, that waking up to sunlight, that climbing a freaking set of stairs, that literally anything, that *life* makes it worse?

The pounding brick image fades, and the all-too-familiar resignation takes over.

This is my life. The pain isn't that bad. I can do this.

I take the first step. The pain pulses higher, harder. I wait for it to fade. Then I take the next step. Again, pain floods my system. But this time it doesn't release.

I can't do this.

I used to dream of doing big things. Of traveling to Australia, of taking road trips from Colorado to Mexico, of building coffee shops for youths to frequent, to be *free.* Instead, I can't climb a stupid staircase.

With gritted teeth, I pull out my cell. Randy answers.

"Can you help me?" My voice cracks. I'm ashamed. I'm embarrassed. I want to hide.

"Yeah, baby. Where are you?"

"On the stairs."

He hangs up and appears seconds later. His face floods with concern. He's wearing an olive T-shirt that brings out his tanned skin and sets his dark eyes sparkling. "Are you okay?"

"I'm stuck." My tone is emotionless. The image of pounding the wall returns.

"Oh, baby." He trots along the stairs and lays a gentle kiss on my forehead. It cuts through the pain, and I yearn to bury myself in his arm. "I'll carry you." He squats in front of me and grabs onto my legs, pulling me onto him piggyback style. He slips his arms through the grocery bag and easily climbs the stairs for both of us.

Once he sets me down, I can't look at him. I stare instead at our hand-me-down couch with sagging cushions. *He didn't sign up for this. He didn't choose to marry this.*

As if he hears my innermost thoughts, he sits beside me and pulls me into his chest. It's thick and solid as an anchor. "I knew you were sick when I asked you to marry me."

I let out a tearless cry. A handful of years ago I didn't need anybody. Sure, I wished I'd brought Kelly to my appointments, but I still managed without her. Now? I can't even manage stairs by myself. My shoulders shake. But even that movement reverberates through my head.

I need to sit.

I need to sit and forget. When the pain eventually calms in the next couple days, I lose myself in art and words, because I'm too numb to do or feel anything else.

21

Growing up, I never had any menstrual cycle symptoms. No mood swings. No cramps. No breakouts. Nothing. I have friends who would pass out in the middle of class because their cramps were so bad. This seems as foreign to me as describing a migraine to one of those miracle people who've never even experienced a headache. So in college, when the first twinge in my lower gut appeared, I thought the eggs I'd eaten for breakfast were undercooked. A little bit of Advil, and I was good to go. Rinse and repeat for a couple months before I realized, *Oh! I've developed menstrual cramps.*

Within six months, the cramps were no longer cramps but Giants Pulverizing My Ovaries.

Head pain I can handle. I'm used to it. There's comfort in a pain you know.

Pain anywhere else in my body throws me for a major loop. Any pain that is not localized in my head is a LEVEL 10 ABORT ABORT.

I spent several afternoons on the floor of my cramped apartment with Randy-the-fiancé holding my hand and his ER doctor daddy on speed dial. Great way to get to know your future in-laws. Highly recommend.

After marriage, I call Randy-the-husband home from class and work for the cramps more often than I do for the migraines. He spends hours alternating between turning the pages of his assigned reading and holding my hand.

Birth control in pill form releases hormones into the bloodstream. Any type of it spikes my migraines within two days, so I can't go near the stuff. When I find out an IUD will not only control the cramping but also only release a localized hormone, I sign up right there in the OB-GYN office.

Inserting the IUD is one of the most painful experiences of my life and almost causes me to pass out.

I have over five years of chronic pain in my back pocket, and yet, for the first three months, my insides are stuck in hell. A constant, piercing-burning penetrates through my lower abdomen into my very center. When you combine that hell with the hell in my head? Hell upon hell upon hell. I can do nothing but curl into a fetal position or, when the burning isn't as intense, paint. Forget writing. I can't focus on words long enough.

How long until my body adjusts to the IUD? The OB says it will take a while, but after three months? Four? Six? Should I take it out? She says to wait a while longer before we decide. So I wait. But it *hurts*. Then if I do take it out, I have to go through the pain of removing the dang thing and the pain of the cramps.

Every choice ends in pain. With no way to win.

Why are my only two choices pain and pain? Why does this seem like such a cruel decision?

One half of me wants to accept the situation, wants to move on in peace by checking off all the good little things they tell you about in Sunday school and on chronic illness blogs: Pray. Meditate. Rest. Journal. Embrace reality.

The other part of me is coated in thick anger. I don't want to look at God. I don't want to pray. I don't want to attend church (as though I can tolerate the stimulation). I don't want to listen to worship music (as though I can tolerate the noise). I don't want to take out a pen and scribble out my emotions. I want to rip my Bible in half.

I launch curse words, I launch *I hate you*s, I launch every weapon in my meager arsenal at the God who won't give me a third option. I enter a state of anger. I'd been angry about pain before. Multiple times. I'd done all the "grieving" steps. Multiple times. But this anger is different. Harder. Sharper.

Desire forms like a cast-iron knot behind my sternum: *I will find a third option.* I will. If anybody could do it, it's me. I'm a lateral thinker. I think outside the box and am not afraid to flip the box upside down. I'm not afraid to play with outlandish ideas. I can do it. *Watch me,* I tell everyone who'll listen.

Some people might think this is blasphemous, that I shouldn't be angry at God, that I shouldn't try to find another way. I don't agree. If God can't take a lick of anger from a hotheaded and hurting twenty-something, then He's not much of a God, is He? Besides, I think God has always prized honesty over pretty words and emotions. I think He'd much rather take my anger and silence, because it's *real*, than fake prayers and platitudes.

Since I don't believe in editing my feelings for God, I let myself burn.

And burn. And burn. And burn.

For six more months, I rail to my friends. I rail to my counselor. I rail to my husband. I rail to everyone except God, because *how dare He*.

I rail until I burn myself out of words.

Until I'm left with only the numb anger.

Still, I've come no closer to finding my third option.

But because I'm numb, I can finally pay attention to the nudging.

There's this concept in creativity called the Muse, the source of creative inspiration. If words flow out easily, the Muse showed up. If you're staring at a blank piece of canvas with no idea what to do, the Muse hasn't arrived yet. If you're walking along the street and a melody pops into your brain, the Muse just gave you a gift. Artists of all mediums treat it more like a person than a concept.

The Muse is the tiny nudge of "use orange instead of red" when you're in the middle of a paint stroke. It's the way your fingers type out "and then the building exploded" at the end of a chapter when you had planned for all your characters to go inside and have a tea party. It's the moment you realize your musical sketch needed a violin performing a counterpoint melody.

You can either choose to follow the nudge or ignore it. It's totally your choice. Sometimes orange is exactly what the painting needed—in fact, it makes the painting. Sometimes an exploding building is exactly what the plot needed. Sometimes the violin counterpoint takes the musical meaning to an entirely new level. Sometimes the nudges are a complete flop, but the payout is always worth the risk. The more you nurture the Muse by obeying the nudges, the more you will notice it, and the more these nudges will pay off.

When God nudges you, it feels exactly the same. Same choice. Same risk. I'd go so far as to say God *is* the Muse. Who's to say He's not?

So when I say I sense the nudging, I mean in the same way the Muse presents a *what if* idea. A tiny little tinkling on the top of my head, more feeling than whisper, a slight sudden knowing of *Yes, orange paint not red.* In this case: *Yes, it's time to face God and face the pain instead of fanning a dying flame.*

All my words are still burnt to crisp, but who needs words?

I take out a shiny new canvas and settle myself into my art space. My head *throb throb throbs* in time to soothing background music. A sliver of light escapes the dark emerald curtains behind me that are closed to prevent light from seeping through. If I feel red, I paint red. If I'm angry, I scribble "I am angry." I slash the canvas. I stab the canvas.

Like the garden, the only rule is: If I feel it or think it, it goes on the canvas.

I let all my anger and frustration out on that 16x16 square of white fabric. All the while, I focus on the word "Why?"

I'm a writer and an artist. I enjoy mystery. I love wonder. I'm one of those weird people who delays opening presents because the anticipation is three-quarters of the fun. The fewer boundaries, the better I do. The more gray area, the more I thrive. I don't need to know what the reason is to live, I'm just happy knowing there is one.

But this time, I need a reason. I need an answer. Over and over again, written in charcoal and colored pencil on the canvas: Why why why. Why are there only two choices? Pain if I leave in the IUD. Pain if I remove it. Why do I have to choose at all?

Until there is another Muse-like nudge from God: "You were never meant to choose."

I slow my brushstrokes and stare limply at the colors swirling on the canvas, pooling in the spots I stabbed. With each further paint stroke, the burning sensation lessens and the numbness wears away. *I was never meant to choose.*

It's not the answer I'm looking for. It's not the answer I want. It doesn't address the *why*. It doesn't even give me hope. But it's *an* answer. A momentary answer for the question I'm truly asking: Why is this happening?

I don't think God intended me to have pain. I don't think God ever *wanted* me to have pain. It's not a part of the original design. But this world is broken. And all of creation is crying for relief, for redemption. Including me.

In the answer, I sense God's grief and his sorrow. An anger, a grief reaching even deeper than mine. I sense Him holding my hand. I sense empathy and sympathy. Not a huge wave of emotion, but another Muse-like nudge. A deeper knowing.

All my questions aren't answered. But this particular one gives me enough peace for the day and until my body eventually adjusts to the IUD.

All these years later, when I seek answers from God, I don't get "the" answer. I get *an* answer for the moment, usually for a deeper question. In that moment, in this moment, an answer is enough.

22

Randy returns from a weeklong retreat with photos of a bunch of men peeing off a cliff, a backpack full of sweaty man clothes, hair that is more grease and grit than actual follicles, and a poem. Somewhere between the late-night conversations and daytime exploring, he had rewritten Psalm 56, a song from the Bible, for me in the framework of my migraines.

I'm open, but I don't talk a ton about what living with chronic pain looks like. Mainly because I've found most people tend to shrink away from the ugly parts of life. And pain is very ugly. I get it. I don't blame them. Nobody wants to be reminded that pain can happen to anyone at any time.

But if you want a small taste of what chronic pain is like, this poem is precious and sweet and scary-accurate as to how I feel much of the time. I love how it ends on a hopeful note. Because when you live surrounded by ugly, you need a glimpse of beauty to keep going:

Be gracious to me, O God, for agony
tramples me,
All day long, pain oppresses me;
My migraines trample on me
without ceasing,
For in hordes they attack me
mercilessly.

When I am in anguish and defeated,
I put my hope in You.
In God whose word I praise,
In God I trust; I shall not be
overcome,
Despite what flesh can do to me.

All day long my migraines cripple
my ambitions;
My body is set against me for evil.
They stir up desire, always lurking,
They prey on my Story,
As they wait to consume me.
From such agony will You free me?
In mercy, remove my pain, O God!

You have kept count of my writings;
You put my tears in Your bottle.
Are they not in Your book?
Then my pain will be healed
In that Day when You come.
This I know, that God is for me.

23

Since I'm no longer working, we earn grocery money by housesitting for my cousins. They have a lovely fireplace that scorches your back in winter months and an artist's dream of a sunroom for the other seasons. I curl on the lounge chair with an ice pack tucked underneath my temple. I haven't yet discovered Audible or the library's hoard of audiobooks, so I turn on my Kindle's speaker function.

I spend hours lying with a blanket over my head, ice under my face, the Kindle microphone pressed to my ear, listening to a story. I'm all for AI voices, but you can only take a couple days of listening to RoboNarrator before you need to scream.

A tiny little nudge tells me to paint. The same type of *use orange paint* nudge. I'm so bored and fed up with RoboNarrator, I decide to listen.

Randy swings by our apartment and hauls over my

painting supplies, helping me set up in the dining room. The light filters in, sending spinning dust motes in the air. The turquoise walls are cheerful and soothing. As I stare at the blank canvas, another little God-Muse nudge niggles at my core.

Paint a migraine.

I've never tried to paint or describe in picture form what a migraine looked like. Like a monster in a horror movie, the worst ones are the evils you cannot name and cannot shine a true light on. The best way I can describe my auras are as "blurry, flashing lights." Just thinking about the aura's shape stimulates enough nausea to force me to glance for the nearest trash can.

The impulse to run away from the monster is strong. But isn't the artist's role to look at the monsters and name them? Which means I bear the call to look at the dark and give it a name, like Meg does in L'Engle's *A Wind in the Door* when she names the Echthros.

I face my monster with steely resolve and try to paint an aura.

I've been painting with watercolors for about a year, but the thin layers of translucent paint don't have the weight I need. I search for another medium and find a box of abandoned acrylics in my cousins' craft room. I've never tried them before. A hard squeeze of the tube, and I glob on layers. Iridescent paints and gold glimmer capture the flickering quality. As I paint the telltale C shape, the nausea grows in my belly. By the end of my painting session, I can't even look at the canvas. That's how I know I got it right. The painting triggers the same physical reaction an actual aura does.

I set the canvas in our apartment hallway. Which means I walk by the darn thing about thirty times a day and get punched with nausea Every. Stupid. Time. After two weeks, I notice I can slide by without the gut-wrenching turn in my stomach. I've become desensitized to the aura.

This is the first time in my life I have had power over my migraines.

I still can't control the pain. I still can't control when the auras arrive. But for a short period of time, I can. When painting, I dictate when the aura shows up. When painting, I dictate how big the aura will grow. When painting, I dictate for how long there is nausea.

A tiny bit of control, and I can dominate the world.

Suddenly, I can show my husband and my family what I experience. The canvas becomes a doorway to share what migraine is truly like for me. I don't understand how much they misunderstood until I have the visual aid. I find myself surrounded with a team of supporters rather than a team of skeptics. Because they understand better, I have actual allies, willing to help me out when I'm down.

I paint more migraines. I experiment with gold and silver and rose foil to get that iridescent quality. I experiment with interference paints and other mixed-media. I can depict the chaos in the colors and the feelings in a way I never could with words. Because, sometimes, words just aren't enough.

Migraine is still the monster in my personal horror

movie. But with brushes and paint, the monster doesn't have to dictate my life's plot anymore by lurking unseen around every corner. I have the ability to cope, to fight back, to turn on the lights and name the monster for what it truly is: an illness that doesn't own me.

24

I'm on the couch watching *Vampire Diaries* with the great dilemma of which ship to root for when my phone rings. The caller ID says MUMZIE. Our apartment is an entire five minutes from my parents. I thought that meant I'd see them weekly, have a spontaneous cup of coffee on a random Wednesday morning, have a closer relationship with them than I did in high school. But my parents are busy. Between grad school, normal family responsibilities, Anna's illness, and my own pain, it's not unusual for nearly a month to go by without seeing them.

I hesitate before picking up. "Hey, Mom."

"Do you want to go shopping with your sisters and me? We're thinking of going to the Nordstrom café for lunch, and you can meet us there."

They have the best sweet potato french fries and the aioli is to die for. I know what this is—a hand reaching out to me.

But I'm tired. And I hurt. And I'm still mad that the last

time I invited her out for coffee, she said no. I'm not normally passive-aggressive, but today the pain stabs and I can't think straight and I don't have the energy to be blunt.

"Maybe next time," I say and hang up.

When I push *play* on the show, I feel the loneliest I have in weeks.

25

I'm twenty-three with nearly six years of the now-named chronic/intractable migraine. We are still in our apartment, though we've recently closed on a house. The floor is caked with flecks of paint that will take two weeks to scrape away before we move. Our living room has wood shavings tucked into the carpet fibers from Randy's creative hobbies. Between the two of us, our space is like a giant art studio. Our shared office space has a cardboard divider with DO NOT CROSS printed in permanent marker to keep Randy's desk crap from migrating onto mine. I'm both excited and intimidated to move into something bigger.

Randy is currently chapters deep into his grad school reading, balancing both school and a job he despises so I don't have to work, while I, yet again, am hours deep into another migraine. This time, it's one of the daily non-aura migraines, like the first time I noticed them in my gen-ed health class, but more severe. They feel the same as the normal aura migraines now, just as sharp, just as overwhelming, except they don't last for days at a time. The tile in our tiny kitchen is cool. I squat there, hands on the cold, staring at the caulk. Tears streak my face. I'm physically stuck. Half my body wants to curl into a ball. The other half wants to reach out and grab the knives sitting a foot away. Use the knives to cut out the pain. Fight pain with pain and shove the blade through my temple.

The suicide thoughts are lifelines, promising me a respite because Christians believe that after death, there is no pain. *You* still exist, your body, though a new version of it, your personality, your soul—everything. You. Without the pain.

It's a glorious and tempting thought. Especially when you're stuck in a place where there is no relief. Historically, suicide was despised in the Christian faith. To murder yourself meant committing a sin that could not be forgiven. Now it is viewed with a lot more compassion and as the tragedy it really is.

But I know how these suicide thoughts work. If I even move my arm in the direction of the knives, I'd start on that slippery slope. The trick to moving past the thoughts is to never move an inch in the direction they're whispering. Otherwise the thoughts will grab you, and, like quicksand, the harder you struggle the faster you sink.

And so I'm stuck. Physically trapped between my two warring selves. An internal battle raging with no outward movement. I cannot move. Should not move. I want to end. I don't want to end. Dear God, what am I supposed to do?

Eventually, Randy hears me crying. He abandons his

reading and pulls me into his lap, legs splayed over our tiny plush mat, through the hours while the pain continues. As the night creeps on, he invents new rules. Whenever I have any thoughts, I have to text him. Any thought, any feeling, any impulse = a text.

We don't lie to each other (except for surprise purposes, which I have absolutely no moral qualms about; I would lie to Jesus Himself if it meant keeping a surprise). If I make a promise, I'll keep it. And I do text. But even with this system in place, more than once I go to cut up an apple and discover he has hidden the kitchen knives so I won't be tempted to introduce them to my temple.

"I have another idea," I say. "How about I get a tattoo?"

We call the tattoo parlor the next morning and set up an appointment. I arrive with the word "story" in Randy's handwriting. The artist paints a 1x3 inch script across the inside of my wrist against the backdrop of a watercolor awareness ribbon for chronic migraine. Even to this day, while the script isn't as sharp as before, I still love it. Now, if I ever reach for a knife, I have to see the word first, and I'll be reminded: Pain is not the end. Pain is part of the bigger story.

Then Randy suggests sending me to pain management therapy to help reduce the suicide impulses.

Dr. M's name is given to us by a reputable source, and she has an opening within a week. She's older with blonde, graying hair and wields vibrant colors and a *talk to me* smile. Until that first session, I don't know how much I need somebody to chat with about my pain in an unfiltered and unbiased way. Randy has been my confidant since the beginning of my pain turning chronic. It's a heavy burden, and he shouldn't have to help me carry this all by himself.

But the sessions quickly turn . . . How do you say *toxic* in a nice way? Dr. M perches on a bright ultramarine chair. She doesn't carry a clipboard but sits with her hands clutching her knees. "How has the pain been lately?"

I tucked one cognac boot behind another and try my hardest to be honest, to not underplay the pain. "It hasn't changed. I've been able to paint more, which is a real joy. But it's been really hard. The pain—"

"You just need to focus more on the positive things."

I stare at her. She gives me a smile as though she just solved all my problems.

She's serious. She's honest-to-God serious.

"What about all the suicide urges?" I ask.

"You just need to work through the thoughts and focus on those positive things."

I try not to gape at her. The only reason I didn't go to pain management therapy sooner was because I had done a fabulous job of focusing on the positive. I'm an extremely optimistic person. Anxiety isn't my struggle, and I'm annoyingly cheerful before 8:00 a.m. A laugh is always on the tip of my tongue. I'm so cheerful, in fact, that I don't know a boat is sinking until I'm already drowning.

I was drowning for a very long time before I realize how much migraine had overtaken my life.

I probably *need* to focus on the negative to advocate better for myself.

Within a single session, I'm being told it's my fault for

having suicide thoughts. It doesn't matter that I'm the one who wanted to reach out for help. Because I still have the thoughts, I failed. Because I still have pain, I failed.

Her words make me uneasy. Something about them doesn't balance right. When I come home to Randy and relay our conversation, he looks up from his homework with a dumbfounded expression. He takes my hands and clutches them to his muscular chest. "That's not true. Do you hear me? That's a lie. Migraines aren't your fault. You didn't cause them. You don't want them. You reached out for help, okay?"

"Okay," I mutter back.

"You shouldn't see her again. It doesn't sound like she knows what she's talking about."

Breaking up with a counselor is oddly like breaking up with a boyfriend. I try to bring it up in our last session, but she drops phrases like, "Don't leave me," and, "We can work through this."

I come home shaky and with heightened pain. The next day, a voicemail waits for me on my phone. I make Randy listen to it. It's from her, apologizing for her actions. I still don't go back.

In four years, I'll be willing to return to pain management therapy. The second time will be much better. We'll use EMDR as a way to follow the pain and draw out exactly what I'm feeling. I'll place buzzers in each palm, and they'll alternate vibrating as a way to stimulate both sides of my brain to encourage neuro-connection. It'll help my brain process and heal, not unlike how REM sleep helps you process your day. My counselor will even incorporate art. She'll bring in a huge pad of paper and watercolors and pencils and crayons and markers. We'll stick the EMDR buzzers in the bottom of my shoes and let me paint a montage of images and feelings in kid-friendly mixed-media tools.

Now with the language of art at my fingers and somebody willing to receive it, I'll voice how trapped I feel, how I need to *get out*. I can reach for something besides a knife.

26

Last week I started reading *Writing as a Way of Healing* by Louise DeSalvo. I'm only a couple chapters in, but I already realize this healing thing is a huge part of why I love writing. As a teen, short stories and vignettes and really bad poetry helped me discover and navigate all my emotions.

I also realized I've barely tapped into writing as an intentional way to process migraine.

So, this past week, I try processing about migraines/pain with haikus and another painting. This haiku is about the actual migraine:

> My flesh and skull have
> ground away to reveal a
> swollen, throbbing heart

This one touches on more of the emotional experience of the pain:

Pain is like being
stranded on the still ocean
with no hope of wind

Another poem:

No one to see a life stifled,
A life stripped of star-song.
No one to see Divinity
Unmoved by scraping cries.
No one to see this silent, holy night
When flesh in lifelong refiner's fire
Finally burns free

27

Gilmore Girls streams from the TV. I sit cross-legged on the floor next to our couch, wearing my painting clothes. They are stiff with a mix of dried acrylic paint and masking fluid, a glue-like substance that helps protect watercolor paper from paint to keep it white. I'm working on a painting for a friend's wedding shower. My water bucket is gray with used water and needs to be dumped and refilled. I can't write due to pain, but I can create in other ways.

My life at this point is fairly monotonous. Write, paint, watch TV, nap. Write, paint, watch TV, nap. So when Anna suggests watching *Gilmore Girls* together, it brings a welcome change of pace to my days.

Lorelai's chatter fills the room, but, instead of watching, I have one eye on my sister.

She sits with legging-clad legs folded underneath her on our hand-me-down khaki couch. She keeps glancing at her phone, as though her friends still in college will keep her updated on their every movement so she can pretend she's still there. She's been coming over more and more recently, taking a bit of refuge in our small apartment.

Our relationship is nowhere close to perfect, or pleasant, but today it is peaceful and enough. I can tell by the way her lips tighten and eyes harden that she has to keep herself in check from the harsh words that rise or the way her mood can plummet any second.

As Lorelai and Rory continue to talk up a storm onscreen, Anna's restless energy rises with them. I don't think she's aware of how much she's projecting into the room. The negative emotion is thick enough to sever. It's like she's being slowly gnawed alive, and there's nothing I can do except help provide a safe space for her to be. I stop painting and begin rinsing my brushes. My watercolor rag is sopping with paint and water.

Suddenly, something snaps within Anna. She jumps up. "I need to go." She snatches her purse and, just like that, is swallowed and gone.

Next week, she'll scream, "I hate you! You don't understand! You're no longer my sister!" I'll seek refuge in a closet to cry. I'll lose her for an entire year, until she's mentally stable enough to recognize that I'm not the most evil person alive.

'Cause that's what illness does: It steals those you love most.

28

My go-to poets are Emily Dickinson, George Herbert, and Rudyard Kipling. I love how Dickinson only needs a handful of words to get across a meaning or a feeling, and she's not pretentious about it. No massive words I need to look up in the dictionary, because I swear my vocabulary has halved over the years. I love Herbert because of the way he combines words and plays with rhythm and structure to add even deeper meaning.

As for Kipling, I've always admired how he can tell a story within a poem. He boils an adventure story until there's nothing but marrow and then manages to make the marrow taste like you're eating an entire flank of steak.

He wrote the poem "The Explorer." There's a line that's totally begging to be on a T-shirt: "Look to the Mountains / What is lost is behind the mountains." It speaks to my white-girl wanderlust love.

But I've always loved the mountains. The far east side of Bakersfield is nestled in the San Joaquin Valley foothills. The sun rose over my mountains every morning. Every day when I drove home from school, from practice, from church, from friends, I drove toward the mountains. I have mountains here in Denver too. I can't see them from inside my apartment, but as soon as I step into the parking lot, they stretch like an arm span across the horizon.

It's not the ridges I love or the way the ranges look like tissue paper pasted in layers against a pale sky, though that view has inspired several paintings. Mountains mean there is something *beyond* them. The ridges and rock are not all there is. I can go *past* them and find something new, something lost.

The mountains are a dreamer's paradise.

Whenever I can't leave my couch for long periods of time, or just grow weary of living within illness limitations, I'll walk fifty feet from my apartment, descending a dirt hill where snakes like to frequent, to the path that runs along the river. I'll sit on a bench and just look.

Looking at the ridges, just knowing there is a *beyond*, a *something else*, can be enough. Knowing there is life and space beyond the square footage of my couch, reminding myself of potential possibilities that someday, *someday* I'll go beyond the ridges, helps me settle into the reality of the present. My life moves slower than an inchworm's pace, but looking at the mountains makes this speed more palatable. They move even slower, on a geologic scale, and yet they're still beautiful.

Then I usually go home, take another abortive, and, if I'm not curled in the pile of sagging couch cushions, add crooked ridges into an acrylic painting.

29

As I write this, my head pulses. Last month I went in for my latest round of Botox. Most people know Botox as the magical potion that wards away your wrinkles. But it's also used as a medical treatment for a variety of conditions, like hyperhidrosis or an overactive bladder. For migraine, it can help block the transmission of pain signals in nerve endings. The thirty-odd bee sting shots allow me to get off the couch. Unlike the media portrayals, I don't look any different, save an inability to wield my eyebrows like weapons.

I know these pulsing warning signs and know I need to stop writing. I'm aggravating the pain. If I don't stop, it will push over the edge, and I will need to take narcotics to focus through my new voice lessons. I enjoy learning another art form. The vibrations of music rattle in my head, helping to distract from the pain. But it only works if the pain isn't so aggravated I can't sing to begin with.

I can't afford to take narcotics for a non-aura anymore.

Not when my body is so used to them. But I want to keep writing. I want to keep working on this new novel.

If I keep pushing, not only will I not be able to sing, but I won't be able to write tomorrow either. Such big consequences for a little mistake.

So I step into the garden instead.

In my mind, I see the iron rod gates of the garden are flaking, and rust pokes through. I grasp the bars, and more chunks of paint slide through my fingers. I'm resistant to being here. The pain is too great, and it keeps tugging me away. Then I smell the roses and am a bit more willing. Through the bars, I can see Him sitting in all white, hands folded in His lap, head bowed.

I push through the gate. Again, it is unlocked.

New flowers are blooming along the pebble path: Orchids and snapdragons, my favorite. I bend to pinch open a pink one, its flower mouth popping open in surprise. I pinch open three more, smiling at the way they gape. Someday, when we own a house, I'll plant snapdragons. They remind me of the long summer days of childhood.

"Good morning," He says as I approach.

I slide onto the bench next to Him. The seat is well-worn by now and fits me perfectly. "Good morning. Did you see how the sunlight plays in patches along the path?"

He laughs, a sound like cinnamon and Christmas. "I designed it that way. Do you like it?"

"Very much. Can I ask you a question? Is this real? I can't tell what's real and not anymore. They blur together like a charcoal smudge. And the longer the pain lasts, the more I can't believe it's real. I can't grab onto it like other physical things."

His face twists into compassion, and He wraps strong arms around me in a giant hug. It's warm in his grip. "My child, my child. You whom I love. Then grab onto Me."

"But is this *real*? Or am I making it all up?"

"What do you think this is?"

"Real," I whisper into His shoulder.

He clutches me tighter. "Then it's real."

30

Our bodies are pretty remarkable. Think about it: We're a bunch of jiggling atoms, both solid and fluid, held together by a mix of magnets and magic. There's an entire universe outside our bodies—from plants to planets, physics says there's always something bigger. But there's a universe inside our bodies too. From platelets to subatomic particles, math theory says there's always something smaller. And both universes have the ability to correct themselves.

Dinosaur-destroying asteroid hit your world? Millions of years pass, but the world eventually blooms again. Hit yourself on a branch? Your body will stitch the pieces together.

We can survive almost anything.

One of the coolest ways our bodies survive is by forgetting pain. Have you ever met a mother who can actually recount every second of the birthing process? All we remember is the joy of holding a new life in our hands. Have you ever met a marathon runner who could recall every moment of the passing miles? All we remember is the thrill of the finish and the wash of endorphins from a job well done. If we truly remembered pain, very few of us would be brave enough to endure birth or run a marathon. The sport and the population would die off and evolution would stand still.

Our bodies are designed to forget pain. It's one of the most basic defense mechanisms.

I've seen this again and again in my life. I'll have a low migraine day and invite a friend over for a cup of tea. They'll settle in over the steaming cup and ask, "How was your week?" I'll honestly answer, "Great!" because today I'm with a friend and drinking a flavorful new loose leaf of lemongrass and rose and all these joyous endorphins are making me soar.

Then I'll hear a cough from the other room. Randy walks in wearing a look of shock, and it's not from the amount of papers he needs to complete to finish grad school. "Are you serious? *Great*? You were on the couch half the week."

But those days are gone and behind me. My eternal optimist self is only aware of the pain I'm experiencing in that moment. I can't remember two days ago, when I slammed my computer shut in frustration because the aura crawled across the words and I had to trade my writing for a binge day of TV and ice packs. I can't remember yesterday, when I exchanged my yoga mat for some sunglasses and a dark room because the five-minute drive to the studio would've tipped me over the edge.

This defense mechanism allows me to live day by day, so that I will actually go out and do things. I'm grateful.

Because I'm in a constant state of forgetting, I have the willpower to paint and write and live.

But this mechanism is just as harmful as it is helpful.

It means I'm never very accurate in my pain descriptions.

"How disabling is the pain?" Dr. Path asks. The question fills the whitewashed room.

I kick my feet against the ground and think of the painting I finished. I think of the small group I attended. I think of the dinner I cooked. I think of the queries I sent out and the chapter I added to my novel. I don't think of the hours spent curled in a corner, sobbing. I don't think of how I can't sit through a two-hour church service. I don't think of how the closest to reading I can get is an audiobook. I don't think of all the suicide thoughts because I just want *out*. I don't think of when I called my husband to carry me up a flight of stairs or how I can't follow the prof's lecture or interact with my small group members or how I can only write for fifteen minutes a day.

All of that is gone. How am I supposed to compare the pain to my normal when I've forgotten what my normal is?

"Maybe a little?" I say. A typical Enneagram seven response, to underplay pain.

This basic human instinct and my tendency to downplay and disconnect from pain work together. Getting the correct treatment is impossible when you're not telling your doctor the entire truth, even if you're not purposefully lying. I think this disconnect is partially personality. I struggle with negative feelings and am quick to rewrap them into something more positive and shiny. The disconnect is also partially because this illness is invisible. I look the perfect picture of health. I act healthy. When I gaze in the mirror, even I can't believe I'm not healthy.

Randy's job is gracious enough with his schedule to accommodate my appointments, and he leans forward now. "No. She's disabled. Can you let her get a parking plaque? Because half the time the fifty extra feet in the parking lot will zap all her energy for the day and make the pain worse. It happened last week on Tuesday."

I slowly learn to combat this forgetting by making better notes in a pain calendar. For years, at least once a week I lay my head on Randy's lap and bury my face in his stomach. "Is this real? Am I making this up? Is the pain this bad?"

He strokes my hair, and his arms tightens around me. "Yes, baby. You're not making it up. This is real. It's this bad." Over and over again, he directs me back to my journals and my pain calendar, where I can see the evidence for myself.

31

Today I crave narcotics.

Dr. Path declares I need to be shipped off to an intensive headache clinic. I should've gone years ago. But I'm not allowed in the intensive headache clinic if I haven't been off narcotics for a period of time, to rule out overuse headache. Then I'll have to wait for an opening, which can take a couple months.

We've been in our new house on the southwest side of Denver for a couple months. It has tall, oversized ceilings in our living room. We paint the walls shades of blue and cover the salmon-hued fireplace with white. A stack of antique trunks stand next to our dining table. I love having a space that reflects more of our tastes.

Now I sit in my new navy armchair, my knees tucked into my chest. My hands are vices around my skull, and all I can think about are those circular narcotic pills. Taking them won't do anything against the pain. They only take the very edge off to make it more bearable. I never once experienced that "high" they talk about in movies. The pills keep adding up as even the sharp edge of pain won't go away and it never stops and I just want relief.

My best chance is the clinic.

I know this, and yet I still can't help but *want* the narcotics.

Anything, anything, to stop the pain.

Today, the pain is mostly bearable. I can probably write a couple scenes in my novel if I try. It's the emotional side that's more difficult. The fact that the pain is *there*. That it's always *there* and will always be *there*.

I can't stand it anymore.

I want it to stop.

Anything to make it stop.

I crawl over to Randy, who is immersed in prepping a sermon. After graduating, he accepted a position as an interim youth pastor for our church. He loves students, loves to laugh with them and hear their stories. We're excited about the potential great fit. I move aside his iPad so I can take over his lap. I rock in-between his arms. The weight of his muscles is soothing.

"It'll get worse before it gets better," he says, running a hand over my spine.

"I know." I burrow my face into his neck to inhale more of his scent. He smells like home, a mix of man and earth and safety all rolled into one. For a moment, the pain lifts and my shoulders relax. Then it's back. "I just want it to stop." His fingers splay across my hair, his thumb dances along the edge of the pain. "Please make it stop," I say. "Please just make it stop."

He tightens his grip on me. "Oh, honey." There's sorrow and regret in his voice, and I know he'd walk to the end of the world barefoot if it meant thirty minutes of relief for me.

He calls into work, tells them he'll be late to a meeting, and sits with me for an hour until I can stop thinking about the narcotics long enough to watch a crappy TV show.

32

When you hear the buzz word "comparison," most people immediately think of scrolling through social media and seeing somebody else's picture-perfect life and comparing it to their own seemingly dull one. If your life doesn't look like theirs, we automatically slap an invalid sticker on it.

When I think of comparison, I compare myself with those who seem sicker than I am. Sure, I'm waiting to be admitted into an inpatient facility. But, oh, they were admitted into the hospital twice? Oh, their Instagram is filled with cut flowers because they can't go outside their garden while mine has a photo of last week's walk? They must be worse off.

And if their version of illness is what illness looks like, then what does that mean for me? Is my illness real? Is this pain real? Should I tell my doctor not to send in my application for the clinic?

The self-doubt is paralyzing.

When I compare, I feed the invisibility stigma: I'm not strong enough, I'm not brave enough, I just need to push through it—it's not real because it's not as visible as the girl with crutches. People are thrilled to tell you the pain is all in your head. Well, it is. The pain is literally in my head. But they like to take a giant eraser and try to scrub it out, as though it were a figment of my imagination. You can't scrub away an amputated leg. It's there. It's in your face. The leg is unavoidably gone.

But you can scrub away hidden pain.

Erase. Erase. Erase.

There are times when having an invisible illness or disability can be helpful. People don't assume I'm sick, so I don't get judged in the same way as somebody with, say, cerebral palsy. I do get a great thrill in dressing up in a cute dress, a killer pair of heels, and then dropping the "I'm sick" bomb. Maybe it's a little sadistic of me. But it's really funny seeing people scramble over their misjudgments. You can read it in their body language. I've had more than one person tell me they first thought I was "bitchy" and "above it all," only to find out later what they read as "bitchiness" was me struggling with brain fog, unable to even follow the conversation. And, they sometimes tack on, I'm easily the weirdest person they've ever met.

Why do I find this so hilarious? Perhaps I have to because otherwise it will hurt.

But in terms of getting taken seriously, having an invisible disability makes asking for help so much harder. Doubly so if you're female. Who will believe you? When they scroll through your social media, you seem as normal as they.

Erase. Erase. Erase.

I have trouble taking advantage of resources meant for those with disabilities. A quick stab of guilt when I park in the handicap spots. Because who will believe me if I voice my pain while laughing with colleagues at the bar? The only person who will see what that hour of laughter has cost me is Randy. While we've gotten slightly better in the publishing world about including racial or LGBTQ+ diversity, we're still way behind on including the disabled community. Especially those who are invisible.

When I scroll through my social media accounts, I'm quick to celebrate other people's book announcements and successes. Then I check my Yearly Goal list and feel terrible for not achieving the same, as though all my success were washed away with the tears of the last migraine.

Erase. Erase. Erase.

Turns out when you're stuck comparing yourself and feeding the stigma, you become invisible to even yourself.

I try to start making myself less invisible by speaking more. By sharing what my life looks like—good and bad. By not using fancy face filters on Instagram Stories. By purposefully celebrating every milestone. By keeping better track of my pain and symptoms so that I can see what I fight through. By not erasing my narrative.

Maybe, with time and practice, I'll eventually stop erasing myself.

33

I hear Randy crying outside.

After the cleaning crew left, he didn't realize he had left the window open to fume out the chemical smell. It's the only way I can tolerate any type of cleaning agent. I'm curled on the couch again, temple pressed against a royal purple pillow. Even with his best efforts, the smell has already aggravated my pain, and I don't have the energy to move. The gnawing want for narcotics has lessened, but that doesn't mean I don't crave for the pain to stop. I don't mean to overhear the conversation with his close friend.

I peek enough to see him sitting in our deck chair, a fire crackling beside him.

"I just can't do it, man. It's so hard. I had to carry her up the stairs again yesterday. She couldn't do it and it just—it just rips your heart out, you know? To hear the person you love most say they wanna die." He wipes a hand across his nose, somehow making sniffling a manly action.

My heart aches, and I curl deeper into the cushions. My tears sting my eyes. I want to cry with him. I want to cry for him. He carries so much. Me, literally, sometimes. There are days I wonder if his life would've been better if he didn't get down on one knee. Should I have said no?

But anytime I mention this to him, he's quick to cut me off. "No. You're still the best thing that's happened to me."

Caretaker burnout is a challenge. Most people focus on the sick one in a relationship and forget to acknowledge the caretaker with more than a pat on the back. They are the true heroes. They experience just as much depression, if not more, than their sick loved one and are often running on fumes—exhausted, overlooked, frustrated. They usually lose friendships because their role as caregiver prevents them from socializing as much. They grieve the loss of dreams as well as the previous relationship they had with their loved one. They often try to make their sick loved one happy and bear the responsibility for the other's emotions, even when this isn't healthy. They forget to care for themselves, taking on burden after burden in silence. And yet the good ones continue loving.

Randy is one of those.

"I'm okay," he says. "Just empty. Work is hard. I'm getting panic attacks every time I prepare a sermon. Yeah, three to four times a week. I don't know what to do. I thought being a pastor was my dream."

A pause.

"You're right. There's something else I could be doing. I just don't know what."

I make a mental note. He's given up so much for me. After the narcotics flush from my system and I come home from the clinic, it will be time for me to help him find his place in the world.

34

I don't think I realized before how much shame and embarrassment surrounds my migraines. I don't feel shame for having them. I can't control it, and they are common enough.

I feel shame for how it affects my life.

I'm embarrassed I can't remember people, their names, and facts about their lives they shared with me in confidence. I can't remember details about people I've known for years. I'm embarrassed I can't remember what I've read half the time. I'm embarrassed because I can't even remember when this symptomatic brain fog started. That photographic memory I was proud of? Yeah. That died.

I'm embarrassed I need my husband to repeat a complex concept four times because I have trouble following. I'm embarrassed I have to stand and pace to get through a church service. I'm embarrassed I can't keep up with friendships and that my social circle has dwindled to a measly puddle. I'm embarrassed I can't hold a normal job, that I binge watch seasons of TV because that's sometimes all I can do for the day. I'm embarrassed I can't muster the energy to go to the grocery store half the time even on a good day. I'm embarrassed Randy continues to carry me up the stairs half the time. I'm embarrassed Randy does most of the life load. (Granted, I've learned to not sell myself short on the things I can contribute to. I keep our calendars synced, keep us on budget, and feed us, and that's no small feat.)

I'm embarrassed I can't stay up late and socialize with everyone at writing conferences. I'm embarrassed I had to try *hard* not to develop a narcotics addiction. I'm embarrassed I pay to attend painting workshops to learn from great artists, only to miss them half the time. I'm embarrassed I don't know how I got here, that I don't remember who I used to be. Sometimes it's like I'm on an island, with no memory of how I became stranded in the first place. All I know is that I'm here and I have to deal with the tropics and starvation and I can't build a fire to save my life.

But I don't want to be embarrassed. I don't want to live my life in shame. I don't want to avoid doing the things my body needs because I'm too ashamed that I need them to function.

Besides, how many of us are *really* looking at the other? We are so caught up in our own embarrassment, many times we miss other people's. And those who do notice and judge... do I really want to be friends with them anyway?

I can either live my life surrounded by this embarrassment. Or I can embrace it and laugh.

I choose not to care. It's a form of enlightenment. It's a form of dissociation. It's a mix of both.

I have to choose not to care every time I do something that can be embarrassing. I hesitate before slipping out the back of a writing workshop class to take an abortive. I hesitate before sticking my Cefaly electrode to my forehead. Even though it's supposed to stimulate the trigeminal nerve bundle to help moderate pain, it looks like a giant metal eyeball that sticks to your forehead. I wrap a head scarf to cover it so I can browse the bookstore with Anna. Every time I go to the movies, I hesitate before bringing out my sunglasses. I'm afraid the teens behind me will secretly laugh. I'm afraid the doctor in the next row will judge.

They might.

But I choose not to care.

I am loved. I am valued. And this is what I need to do to take care of my body.

Screw it.

I shove the glasses on and pull on my best movie star attitude.

Besides, those teens behind me don't know I'm not one, right? And aviators reek of confidence.

Of course, I'm still working on this. I'll interrupt Randy mid-conversation when my brain fog is so thick I can't follow what he's saying, but I don't dare do anything else but fake smile and nod when engaging someone else. I'll wear Cefaly uncovered with my friends in private, but I'm still too embarrassed to wear it in public when I actually need it most.

Baby steps. One pair of aviators at a time.

35

Anna's writing a book.

We sit together in our local bookstore, The Tattered Cover. The seats are eclectic and comfy, and their chai is the best I've ever had. I love wandering the shelves and running my hands over the spines, imagining the day my book will be among them. I've been here so often I recognize each staff member.

Writing is easier at home, but this is my attempt to continue repairing my relationship with my sister. We have more in common now that she is finally done with college. We both have significant others, we both try to cultivate writing as a habit, we both have names for our illnesses, and we both struggle with FOMO as others blaze ahead in life.

Illness has finally equalized us.

Our respective manuscripts are on our little table, and pen ink stains our fingers. The narcotics have cleared my system by now, and last week my neurologist sent in my application for the clinic. I wish I could say I feel "cleaner," but mostly I tear at my nails, refreshing my email twenty thousand times a day to see if there's any response from them.

Anna stops spiraling when she writes. She seems almost herself as she pieces together her narrative forms. She even cracks a joke. She is currently an MFA student. Her project is a memoir about bipolar, body image, and spirituality. I think it's brilliant. So far, my favorite line is when she calls me a "she-demon." I think when it's published I'll print the phrase on a T-shirt.

I scrape my pen across my paper to circle a typo. If I look deep enough inside, I realize I'm jealous. I researched the disability MFA programs of several graduate schools, only to close out of the website pages. I even reached out to the staff of one. I quickly realized: Even with a modified program, I wouldn't be able to keep up.

But as Anna talks about what she's learning, a streak of pride fills me, even as I duck lower to hide the Cefaly neuromodulator pinned to my forehead from a passerby. I've been trying to study writing on my own, scouring YouTube videos, reading and studying books, attending free online writing conferences, reading summaries of paid conferences, even throwing in some cash to attend a *Writer's Digest* workshop. At one point, I win a free ticket to attend the Rocky Mountain Fiction Writer's Colorado Gold Conference. My notebooks are filled with advice from workshops and keynote speakers. After attending, I crash the next two weeks.

But I've been learning the exact same things as Anna. My self-led learning is paying off.

She hands me her newest chapter. Her hands shake from a medication side effect, but she fights through it. I squint through the head pain to read her words, knowing the effort will aggravate the pain. She's almost smiling, so I smile back and try.

36

Sometimes I am only a brain. The rest of my body has ground away underneath my throbbing skull.

I have lots of ideas inside my brain. The poem I wrote yesterday. A collage of images to illustrate a picture book series. A five-minute animation sequence that would pair beautifully with the song I just heard. The faint melody of a violin waiting to be expanded into a full song.

Each idea has its heartbeat. They each add to my own echoing *wagooshing*, add to the grinding that wears away the rest of my skin and bones.

Today, traveling the flight of stairs separating me from my art loft is as intimidating as my future dream of hiking my first fourteener. Even the decision to go to the movie theater, or to attend my yoga class, or to drive the three-minute distance to pick up my on-hold library books is like felling a dragon.

My heartbeat says, *Please, no, please, no, not today, please.*

And so my house becomes a skull. And I am still the brain trapped inside.

37

I have paint on my hands as I write this. Speckles of fire colors from a cotton shirt I am painting since I couldn't write earlier. It says, "Fire Breathing Bitch Queen," a reference to the *Throne of Glass* series by Sarah J. Maas. I let myself sink into the comforting strokes of the brush. Eventually, I heat up tomato soup and freeze in front of the microwave. Half my vision just blinked out. A month ago, I had twenty-five auras in ten days. A massive intractable attack that could only be stopped with a heavy dose of steroids. Some of those days started like this, with a quick flicker and a vanishing.

My body is tense and I am wary and my muscles are sore from clenching. My vision returns, and all seems well. I grab a can of soda. Now the pain mixes with dizziness and pushes against my frontal lobe, and it's easier to handle. I switch mediums; back to my laptop. I'm making great progress on this new novel, and it's hard to stop when the pain crescendos again. Then back to painting. Back to being kind to my body, to practicing grace.

This morning, I read some articles about different types of head disorders, such as retinal migraine or cluster headache. Maybe I've been misdiagnosed. Some of my actions don't match up with the majority of migraine patients—those who want a dark room to sleep in. I thrash, I moan. I'm restless in my pain. "Active" patients like this are more likely to struggle with suicidal thoughts. Makes sense.

But it also gives me hope. If I truly had been using my narcotics wrong, the clinic will give me a new strategy. I glance at the map calendar above my desk. It's been a month since we sent in my application. My acceptance call should come any day now.

ATTACK

This stage is most associated with migraine—head, pain, throbbing, stabbing, sobbing. For me, it's the longest part of the migraine, lasting days or weeks or longer. It's painful, a rebirthing, and you don't know who you're going to be on the other side. But as the saying goes, "The only way out is through."

Now that you have your sparkly idea—now, now comes the hard part. The meat of the creative process. Sometimes it's easy. Sometimes it sucks. But the only way to finish is to sit and do the damn work, whether it takes days or weeks or longer. You don't know what will wait for you on the other side, if the project will be the same one you started with—or if you will be a completely different person because of it.

Genesis 1:3b
"… And there was light."

38

My version of the Hogwarts acceptance letter is receiving the Headache Clinic welcome packet in my email. After being successfully weaned off narcotics, after juggling insurance and patient forms, there's an opening, and I'm accepted as a patient. I read the instructions and "What to Expect" papers over and over again.

Randy takes me to Target, the muggle version of Diagon Alley, and we load up on needed supplies for my time away. Comfy socks. Easy pull-on sports bras. Star Wars T-shirts. Flowery coloring books with encouraging phrases. Randy spends an astonishing amount of time finding the perfect set of colored pencils.

My bag is packed, and I'm ready to go. I fly early to Michigan (Randy is coming later) and wait at a friend's house in Grand Rapids for the spot to open. Since everybody spends different lengths of time at the clinic and beds are limited, there's no guaranteed date of entering. You go in when someone leaves. I'm tempted to tell Randy to stay home, but I remember the lance I felt in my chest after I told Kelly to stay behind. See? I'm learning. I'm growing.

When he finally arrives, the gratefulness I feel is overwhelming.

I wait almost two weeks before a bed opens. I pressed the pause button on my life, save for the shiny new publishing contract in my inbox for the novel I'm so proud of. My heart burns, and I want nothing more than to sign and commit to publishing a book, but I'm afraid I won't be able to deliver. I remember all the times I've canceled events, walked out on my siblings' graduation ceremonies, said no to wedding invites, promised to show up and couldn't. I can't afford to backtrack on my promise this time. So I press pause on the contract until I can talk with the clinic's doctors.

Nervous and anxious, I hop in the scarlet rental car, while Randy says goodbye to our friend, and wait to drive off into the sunset with the clinic in the distance.

39

"I have loved the stars so fondly to be fearful of the night."

This quote is often attributed to Galileo but is actually the last two lines from Sarah Williams' poem *The Old Astronomer*.

To me, the quote means we don't need to be afraid of the dark times in life.

The following is from *Walking on Water* by Madeleine L'Engle:

> "Milton could have retreated into passive blindness and self-pity instead of trying the patience of his three dutiful daughters and any visiting friend by insisting that they write what he dictated. Beethoven could have remained in the gloom of silence instead of forging the glorious sounds which he could never hear except in his artist's imagina-

tion. Sometimes the very impetus of overcoming obstacles results in a surge of creativity."

If Milton remained afraid of his blindness and never faced it, we wouldn't have *Paradise Lost.* If Beethoven cowered in response to his deafness, we wouldn't have Symphony No. 9 in D minor. Instead, they embraced the stars so fiercely night no longer had a hold on them.

Sometimes I'm brave enough to continue writing, to continue painting, to continue living. Sometimes I wish I could pull an *It's a Wonderful Life* and zap my life with some angel power and an amazing soundtrack and see how my bravery to keep going has changed my surroundings. To my great dismay, life isn't a movie and I don't have an epic soundtrack following me everywhere. I might never know. But that doesn't diminish the validity of clinging to the stars.

What are the stars?

That which is true, pure, beautiful, just, excellent, honorable, admirable, praiseworthy.

Milton and Beethoven's work totally qualifies as hitting all of these. Even if you're not a fan of theirs.

This doesn't mean we deny the power or the existence of the dark.

Of pain. Of failure. Of rejection. Of lack. Of emptiness. Of death.

But we have permission to no longer be afraid of it.

Yeah.

I almost believe it.

As we drive through twilight toward the clinic, the first

twinkle of stars appear and the moon is glistening full. Honestly, I'm *terrified* of the dark times. I'm *terrified* of pain. I'm not afraid of death, but I'm *terrified* of dying. I'm so terrified I'd rather be blind about the future. If I ever visited a carnival with my best friends and met a fortune teller, you better believe I'd run the hell away. I have no moral qualms about hamstringing my besties and leaving them to deal with her.

That which is true, pure, beautiful, just, excellent, honorable, admirable, praiseworthy doesn't make the dark go away. It doesn't speed up the rotation of the earth and make the night end faster. It doesn't take away the impact—

Of pain. Of failure. Of rejection. Of lack. Of emptiness. Of death.

It doesn't remove my terror. Doesn't remove my fear of what will happen at the clinic. Does this mean the statement is false?

I don't think so. I may have permission to not be afraid, but I think fear's gonna be my shadow until I finally finish the dying process and, you know, die.

But perhaps like real stars themselves, these stars can help guide me through it.

40

The clinic has a scent. Not the sharp scent of bleach or the stale air normative to hospital rooms, but, like, no-scent. As though all the smells have been vacuumed out. An anti-scent. Which makes sense, considering scent can be a massive trigger for migraineurs, and the staff wants to keep the clinic as trigger-free as possible.

"The kitchen is here. Help yourself to whatever's in the fridge, anytime. We're not trying to keep you prisoner. There's even a lunchroom where the staff eat. You're more than welcome to bring your food and eat there." The nurse is cheery and wearing bright scrubs. She points in every direction, showing me and Randy around the clinic wing of the hospital. "You can even walk the path around the hospital! In fact, we encourage it, if you can. Do as many normal things as you can manage."

I've never been very good at sitting in a chair for several hours at a time, let alone staying put in a hospital room. I'm sure I'll be one of their patients who puts in a good mile every day. Good thing I brought a pair of walking shoes.

I look up and down the hallway. The clinic is set up dorm-room style, with nice-for-a-hospital carpet lining the hallway, scarily reminiscent of my college years. Each person has their own bathroom, and there's a community room at the end of the hall. Unlike college, most doors are shut. Nobody wants visitors.

Randy squeezes my hand over and over as we step inside my room. It's both larger than I expected and smaller than I hoped. There's enough space for a modern gray couch for Randy to sleep on. How are we not supposed to go crazy in such a small space? *I'll just go walking every day. Get some writing in.* I still haven't signed that publishing contract, but I can get a jump-start on revisions and sign it as soon as I return home.

I didn't know then that, not only would I never step on the path, I would not even keep my blinds open to *see* the path. I didn't know I wouldn't touch my laptop except to pull up Netflix. I didn't know I'd barely leave my bed for the entire two weeks.

The nurse pats the bed. "Come on up and roll up your sleeve."

I obey. The bed is surprisingly comfortable considering the context. The nurse inserts what will become my first permanent IV line. I've gotten IVs before. Always for short medical treatments, or a saline solution; nothing that lasted longer than a couple hours max. There's something very different about an IV line that will be with you for over a week. The thought of having a tube enter my vein gives me shivers. It feels as intimate as sex.

She has to get a smaller tube for my veins. They like to play hide and seek with desperate nurses. If I take anything out of this experience, it's how much I hate IV lines.

The nurse explains the protocols, the midnight EKGs, my personalized whiteboard with a list of my medications and abortives with a full description of what they all do, the daily meetings with the team of doctors. Then the question: "So how would you describe your pain level now from 1-5?"

I'd answer that question at least fifteen times a day for the next two weeks. I glance at the pain chart. "Uh, a four?"

"Great! Let's try this abortive." She takes my blood pressure and other vital signs and hands me my first abortive of my clinic experience. When she leaves, I glance over to find Randy popping open a brand-new can of Clorox Bleach wipes. He drops to his knees and starts scrubbing the ground.

"Babe," I say. "They clean in here once a day. It's already sparkling. We're not in a third world country."

"There's still germs, Abby. *Germs*." He doesn't look at me but pulls out another wipe. "I am not walking around here in my beloved slippers until I *know* it's clean."

I get the sense cleaning is his way of reassuring me that everything will be all right.

Ten minutes later, the nurse returns to check on me. The pain has receded a little.

Maybe I don't belong here after all.

After the room is cleaned to Randy's satisfaction, I start

meeting the other patients. A round, older woman arrived the day before me. A dark-haired young man in his thirties has been here a week. One woman, as tall as me but about half my width, nears the two-week mark. She has a migraine mutation called vasospasm. It sounds awful and painful, and I want no part of it. The girl next door is only twelve. She's been chronic for the last five years. Her mom tells me she's barely been able to go to school. I give her my Harry Potter coloring book.

The graying lady in her fifties across the hall receives the "miracle migraine protocol." She walks around with an abortive pain patch stuck to her forehead. I'm not nearly as embarrassed about my Cefaly anymore. She still has pain, but it's more manageable. I expect the same will be for me. She leaves within four days.

Randy and I continue rotating through audiobooks, coloring books, and gluten-free cheeseburgers. I keep taking my abortives and protocols and doing my EKGs.

When my turn arrives to try the "miracle migraine protocol," within thirty minutes my pain forces tears to my eyes. Surely this pain is caused by a pro soccer player aiming kicks at my head, not the medicine. But the pounding doesn't stop. It won't stop. It will. Not. Stop. We run through all my allocated abortive mediations. None of them works.

"How would you describe your pain level now?"

When the doctors want to try again with the miracle migraine treatment a day later, just to make sure my reaction wasn't random, I cry. I know it won't work. I try it again, and I'm right.

Besides the whole forgetting pain mechanism, the other biggest coping trick humanity has is distraction. If you're in the middle of a brain-splitting migraine, listening to an audiobook leaves a trail of story breadcrumbs for you to follow. The pain isn't as overwhelming because you're so excited to see where the breadcrumbs lead. Conversation and to-do lists work the same way. You're so focused on what's outside your body, you don't realize what's going on inside.

Except when you're in a clinic whose sole purpose is to *not* distract you from the pain—in fact, they *want* you to pay attention to it and give them every single detail. The pain dries up your bones. It's like you removed the veil from your eyes only to find yourself in the middle of a desert. Nothing but a dry-cracks land with dust for miles. No end in sight.

Without the breadcrumbs of life reminding me to pay bills, write a scene, get some exercise, cook dinner, I look up and realize just how far away from home pain has brought me.

Randy has to return to work at the church; my final distraction is leaving me alone. He'll be back as soon as he can. I thought I could handle being alone. When I'm at home, solitude is easy. But this type of solitude? With pain as your only companion?

Every single patient in my hall is lost in their own lonely desert.

I belong here. I just don't believe it yet.

41

Right before I leave for the clinic, a stranger tells me, "It must be so nice to have vacations every other day!"

Anybody with a chronic illness has gotten this statement at least once or twice. It takes all your willpower not to throw your water bottle in their face. When I have to take a half day, an entire day, or more from creating due to a migraine, it's not truly a day off.

At the beginning of each year, I sit with a blank sheet of paper and plan out my goals. Then I axe them by two-thirds because, you know, illness. I take the remainder and break them into months, break them again into weeks. Some of my deadlines are from an editor. Others are self-imposed because I'm Type A and have a grand map of my life and need to keep driving if I want to hit all the places I dream to go. I truly don't understand how some people can wing through life without a plan. It could be a side effect of chronic illness. If I don't plan and prioritize and break the task into actionable pieces, it'll never happen. Which means there's usually a to-do list hanging over my head that I'm actively ignoring for the grander purpose of *health*. If I don't take the day off now, my body will respond with upping my pain for an entire week or more later.

It's a weird sensation. Half of you wants to roll over and run away from the pain. You *want* to take the time off. You *want* to stop fighting through the pain for a bit. The other half of you wants to keep working. There's purpose in the work; it's beautiful, and the images and the colors flutter inside like another heartbeat. The push-pull tugs on my emotions, like a rubber band stretching from one side of my rib cage to the other, with all the frustration when the band doesn't quite stretch all the way. It's really hard to describe this dichotomous yearning to someone who only lives for the weekend.

On these "days off," when I'm not forced to cancel plans due to migraine, I'm not only wrestling with pain and other symptoms but this weird mix of frustration and emotion of not being able to do what I really want to do. A day off is no vacation.

Just like my stay in this clinic is no vacation.

A vacation for me is time with no deadline, no to-do list, no true purpose. A vacation is a time to be curious and play. To explore whatever interests me in the moment. To pick up a book about Genghis Khan or research the toilet habits of people in the seventeenth century. To take a short stroll along the fall colors without the responsibility of walking dogs. To go to a beach and squish soft sand between my toes.

To try a new yoga class I have no business being in. To watch a TV show or catch up on cartoons I fangirl over with the ten-year-old neighbor. To sit in a coffee shop and read, just because I like the vibe of the store and the warmth of a mug in my hands. To go to a bookshop and spend an hour touching the bumps of spines and picking one at random.

I need these vacation times for my sanity, to refill my creative bucket, to be a better human. Vacations can span anywhere from two weeks at a beach with an umbrella drink to a single four-hour block in my house where I can let go of stress. I'm a much better spouse if I get out of the house and turn off my phone for a couple hours. I'm a much better creator if I've practiced releasing stress and listening to what my soul needs. I'm a much better migraineur if I can escape its grip.

I cannot be curious during the forced times off. I cannot play—not true play, at least. Most of the time, the only thing I'm listening to is the groaning of my body. I cannot let go of stress, because my entire body is in stress. I'm not enjoying the simple pleasure of watching burnt umber seep into a patch of cerulean. I'm resting because I can literally do nothing else, and the entire time I'm frustrated I'm not downstairs working on my novel edits.

Part of this frustration is my fault. I tend to obsess over what I should be doing rather than being in the moment of what I can do. Most of the time, I try to see those forced days off as chances to do things I wouldn't normally—like listen to an experimental audiobook or a new podcast or that documentary that's been on my list forever.

But it feels different.

When I do return to the computer to edit, I'm restless. My heart hasn't recovered. And it's like forcing my hand to a burning steering wheel with my brain screaming, *Drive drive drive.* But my heart is going, *Not yet, please. This body needs more time.*

Sometimes I ignore my heart. Sometimes I just have to get it done because of that deadline or that bill written in vibrant cruel red. Sometimes the to-do list seems so impossibly long that if I don't tackle it *right now this instant*, I swear it will rise up and strangle me. This usually results in a tug-of-war of creative control. The car wobbles, constantly jerking from side to side, and it takes me a lot longer to reach my destination and puts me at severe risk of an accident.

Most of the time I eventually crash.

If I can give myself more grace, treat my heart with gentleness, the next time I can get behind the wheel all of me is onboard and can go farther. I may not get in as many cars. I may not hit as many destinations. But my hope is that my car won't get stuck and the journey will be worth it.

42

In John Green's *The Fault in Our Stars*, the main character Hazel talks about pain scales. We both hate them because pain is relative. Most are based on a ratings factor from 1-10, with 10 being the worst imaginable pain ever. Your 3 could be someone else's 8. But because they are at an 8 and you're at a lowly 3, you don't get the same treatment or urgency.

It's harder for those with severe pain, because their 3 needs just as much attention, but nobody is looking at *why* their 3 is a 3. Especially when pain is constant. It becomes a backdrop similar to traffic noise. After a year of living in your new house, you think your backyard is a quiet refuge fit for a fairy-tale, until you step outside during rush hour and are hit with the mad horns of angry drivers. And when you add that forgetting mechanism back in, then, well, that explains a lot.

In essence, the 1-10 scale isn't reliable and should be shoved into the disposal. But I digress.

The clinic explains their pain scale of 1-5 is not only

determined by how much pain you're in but on your functioning in that moment, including fatigue.

I love that. This scale is way more accurate. The sheet describing the numbers isn't all that helpful, but when Randy eventually returns, we will shut the door to my little room and spend hours tailoring my criteria for each of the numbers. Now, I can more accurately portray my "pain level" due to a list of specific actions of what I can and cannot do. I can truly track improvement.

Except: categorizing pain can still be confusing. Yes, I *can* write. That would put me at a level 2, right? Except after a twenty-minute writing sprint, I need an abortive and to lie down and watch Netflix and/or stare at a wall. So that means I'm closer to a level 5, right? Except I *can* still write. I can force myself to write. So, back to a level 2?

See where categorizing pain can get hard? Then add doing it in the middle of a hard case of brain fog.

I'm learning to ask: "Yes, I *can* do this. But if I had no responsibilities or to-do's or pressure, *would* I do this?" Usually, the answer is no.

And then there's the whole level 6 question.

When the nurse first hands me the sheet at the clinic, I point to the blank space underneath level 5. "But what about when our pain hits a 6? Is there a category for that?"

The nurse stares at me blankly. Leave it to the artist to ask an out-of-the-box question. "Honey, there is no level 6."

But there is. There is a level 6. Because there are times when I meet all of the sheet's and my own criteria for being a level 5, and yet still have experienced categorically worse pain. An off-the-charts, I'm-going-to-die level 6. I've probably only had twenty of them in my life. Like Hazel's level 10. She never uses her 10 on a pain scale, saving it for a time when she experiences a pain that's uncategorizable. But I don't want to save my top level like she does. It means I can't use the rest of the scale as accurately.

If there's no level 6, it means the days I have to ask Randy what paint colors make green because I can't remember aren't very severe days. They are only moderate. If there's no level 6, it means the days I block out pain to write means the pain isn't as bad as I think it is. It means I've been wrong this entire time.

No level 6 means the pain isn't real. It's not really that bad.

For now, I'm on the floor of my room, my head pressed into the clean fake wood texture. I'm trapped and am so out of control. I can't reach the pull-cord to call for a nurse. Am I even at a 5 yet? Am I supposed to wait until blood leaks from my ears? How do I know if this is the worst pain? I've had worse. Does this mean I don't deserve an abortive, if it can get worse?

If I'm a sonnet, where are my boundaries? Where's the rhyme scheme for me to live by?

Inch by inch, I drag myself across the floor. Anytime I move or think, an axe-like blow cuts through my head. It's raw and blinding, and my sense of space stretches. I'm slipping along a never-ending slope, and I need to hold on and hold on but there's nothing to hold on to. No art here. No stories here. No husband here in this dark pit. Only the faint sense of God's grief reaches me, and I can't hold onto that because it isn't solid. It's not *enough*. It's only been me, only ever me carrying this, and I'm falling and there's no end, not even death, no end no end no—

Time distorts, and crawling takes a lifetime. I pull the cord, and the movement drains me.

The nurse on duty comes in, rushes to my side, helps me up, and stays the next several hours rotating my ice packs. She holds my hand, bringing me orange sherbet to cool the inside of my mouth, whispers assurances, until the raw edge of pain is coaxed down so I can breathe.

"Is this normal?" I whisper through the tears. "Am I at a 5 yet?"

She gives me a new ice pack and dampens a washcloth for the places the ice pack doesn't reach. "You've reached 5 a long time ago."

There has to be a level 6. There has to be.

Otherwise, I'm making this all up. But I'm not. I'm not.

Please, God, I'm not.

43

One of my favorite things about the clinic is its multidisciplinary approach. Most therapy places take one approach: Western medicine or Eastern medicine. Analyzing food, exercising more, or something else completely different alone will not cure it. The clinic emphasizes there is no single solution to controlling migraine. There's no cure. You can only manage. And the best way you can manage is by combing through twenty different approaches, and somewhere in that Frankenstein mix is a multi-combo that can help you.

I really appreciate this approach. I'm also multidisciplinary. I don't love one thing, I love several. I love painting and music and writing and the ache of tired muscles after a long walk and the burn of my belly after a good laugh. If I am so complex, then perhaps my disease is also.

The clinic prepares daily workshops for us to attend. Most patients try to come, to shuffle out of their doors and along the hallway into the common area. But often the pain is too much. You're encouraged to attend, just to get you to move and live a little. There's no shame if you can't.

One class is dietary focused. The nutritionist hands out charts and goes over potential food triggers for migraines, with the true emphasis on eating a balanced amount and variety. What you put in can affect your body. I've been doing dietary trials since junior high and am familiar with almost everything she says. The satisfaction is like a pat on the back: I've already been doing this part right.

Another class is about exercise. We brainstorm different ways we can move despite the pain. Too often I think inside the box when it comes to exercise: jogging or weightlifting. I don't think about other options, such as biking, playing with the dog, yoga classes, even walking around the mall if I happen to be out.

We also take time to mourn the exercise we used to do before the pain took over. I used to be a runner. I was one of the crazy people who loved the ache in my legs as I hit the upper miles. I still love the fresh air and the way it freezes my thoughts into focus. I haven't run in ages. I used to enjoy working out. To have sweat dripping from my sports bra and know it meant I did a good job.

I've lost so much muscle that when I try to lift two-pound weights I have to take a nap afterward. It feels as though I've lost a part of myself.

Another class is about the Spoon Theory. There are websites and many Tumblr pages devoted to discussing this theory, but the idea is new to a lot of the patients. The Spoon

Theory shares how people with chronic illness, or any sort of disability, have less energy than the average person. If energy were measured in spoons, then an average person might have ten spoons of energy. A person who is chronically sick might only have three spoons per day. And a trip to a library might cost all three spoons, while the average person only has to pay one.

In fact, right before I write this, I just got back from the library. It sucks all my energy to get in the car and drive five minutes away, park the car, walk up a flight of stairs, return some books, check out others, walk downstairs, get in my car, and drive the five minutes home. I deserve an award for that freaking marathon.

In this class, the therapist spreads a heap of spoons along the table. Silver spoons, tarnished spoons, wood spoons, teaspoons, ladles, every sort of spoon-shaped object you can find at a garage sale. We pick out the spoon that most represents our life. I gravitate toward a sugar spoon. It's wooden and hand-painted with layer after layer of color, like a rainbow bent into a circle. To me, my spoon represents the art I cling so hard to.

We actually tackle art in two of the workshops. We color on printed pages, which I'm already doing in my room. The next time, the therapist brings in boxes of beads and stones. We string them onto chains. Now, whenever we are in pain, we can run our fingers over the smooth stones and use them to help center our breathing. Like a rosary, we recite meditative statements. At the center of the chain is a special bead, a type of medallion.

I pick out a tiny silver sea turtle.

I spent a holiday in Hawaii a handful of years ago, after I turned chronic but before I realized how traveling affected my body. Half the time I sat on the beach with a towel over my head to prevent sun damage, which I know defeats the tanning purpose of a beach vacation. The other half I spent in the water with a too-tight snorkel mask strapped to my face, searching for sea turtles. When I finally found one, I trailed behind it for two hours. The turtle's flippers rose and sank on the current, up and down, completely unhurried with no care for my inner urgency. Whenever I need to calm myself, when the pain gets so bad I start hyperventilating, I time my breathing to the memory of its flippers rising and falling.

My absolute favorite workshop is the therapy dog. Imagine a group of twenty people, all in terrible pain, all looking like they've been dragged through the deepest levels of hell, all huddled around the small blanket where the dog is allowed to sit. If harvested, this hopeful energy could fuel a city.

The therapy dog is a fat black lab. We all crowd around him, trying to get some of that inherent animal love. But there are too many of us and only one of him. I want to smuggle the dog back to my room, drag it into my bed, and whisper all my frustration into its ear. I want it to lick my palm and take the pain away. I want it to nuzzle me and help me forget.

It prefers the twelve-year-old girl over me. Yes, I'm still slightly upset about that. Yes, I'm aware it's petty.

Sitting with the clinic's lab reminds me of how much I love my own therapy dog. His name is Apollo. He's an Irish-doodle whose only proclivity for hunting is hunting flies. We have another pup, Athena, an adopted Goldendoodle. She's Randy's buddy and would rather help him carry dead tree branches across the yard and dig up sprinkler lines than snuggle for an hour. But Apollo curls underneath my desk while I write, sits underneath my easel while I paint, lays on my feet while I read. He's with me every moment of the day. He crawls into bed with me and won't move until I do. He'll nuzzle my thigh and indulge in a Netflix binge and let me thread my fingers through his hair. Even if the pain forces me to the bath for an hour or more, he'll lay faithfully next to the tub. Periodically, he'll peek over the rim and make sure I'm all right.

Dogs are the superheroes of pain. They are the best distractions, the best comforters, and they never ever complain. I know Apollo is only a dog, but he makes me feel seen better than any prescription med, better than any doctor. Everybody who is sick should have an animal to love and to love them.

44

I've only ever been called out once as being in pain. I showed up for dinner at a writer's conference a couple years ago, so proud that I had taken a nap and an abortive to try to hear the speaker. An older gentleman sat next to me. Near the end of the meal, when everyone quieted to hear the keynote, he leaned over.

"You're in pain, aren't you?"

I sat straighter, shocked. Nobody. Ever. Can see my pain. The truth certainly wasn't written in lines on my face. Botox took care of that. "How did you know?" I whispered back.

"It's in your eyes."

I really wish I had asked him if he had pain too. You only know where to look if you've been there yourself.

Whenever I meet somebody who is sick, it's like stripping off Bruce Wayne to reveal Batman underneath. Here in the clinic, there are many superheroes. There's always a quiet moment that passes when you see underneath the alter ego. A question hangs: Should I tell? Will you reject me? Will you banish me from the city I've fought to protect?

Once the phrase, "Me too," is uttered, the curtain parts and you can skip straight from small talk to shoptalk. You can say whatever you want. Neither of you will share the other's secret. And now you've found an ally to combat alongside you. A DIY Avengers team.

On a sweaty summer day in July, my high school tennis coach pointed to the brick wall hemming the courts and shouted, "You can bust through that wall if you wanted. All it takes is tenacity." Then he made us do pushups against the wall, imagining what bursting through stone is like.

I've never burst through a brick wall, but I definitely feel like I have. Living sick is breaking through a brick wall every day. I am tenacious. I am a superhero. My plainclothes is a strange mix of vivid colors, unreasonably eye-catching shoes, and my favorite mascara brand. My costume is sweatpants, and my mask is three-day-old greasy hair. My secret workshop isn't filled with bot gadgets and a flashy car, but bath bombs and a laptop filled with stories and a loft stuffed with a myriad of art supplies. My Alfred is my husband and my closest friends and the strangers I meet, who all gather alongside me for the fight.

And often my body is the victim, the hero, and the villain, all rolled into one.

45

Two weeks pass of cheeseburgers, closed blinds, thoughtful nurses, and new friends rotating in and out. The group of doctors I meet with every morning believe I have an evolved type of migraine that includes vasospasm.

There's no way to test for vasospasm, especially since migraine with vasospasm is pretty much unresponsive to normal treatment. The only way to tell for sure is if we treat the vasospasm with meds and see if the migraines respond. Even though I can do this at home, this process can take six months. Maybe longer. And even then, getting the vasospasm under control won't stop the migraine. Just help manage it. But I have no other choice.

Not only do I belong in the clinic, but I am, in fact, a difficult case. There's nothing more they can do for me.

Let me be clear, the clinic is a fantastic place. The nurses are so kind. So thoughtful. And, honestly, a joy to be around. The doctors are thorough and take my concerns into consideration and are willing to answer any question, however long the answer takes. Even when they tell me I still have a long way to go, they give hope: There's a new class of medications coming out! However, these meds won't release for another couple of years.

If you've been in and out of doctor's offices much, you know this consideration and thoughtfulness is a golden treasure.

But it's time for me to go home.

Before I'm released from the clinic, I'm scheduled to spend some one-on-one time with their psychologist. Randy returns, and we compile a massive list of questions and concerns I've been stockpiling, including: Do I sign this publishing contract for my novel? We prioritize each topic to optimize my time and go through a quiz to figure out how depressed I am.

My score comes back "moderately depressed."

Yeah.

I could've told you that.

The psychologist is a tiny woman. Even after losing so much muscle mass, I can easily stuff two of her in my body, and Randy has to be careful not to break her hand when he introduces himself. There isn't quite enough room for all three of us, but if I sit on the bed and roll up my legs, we stand a chance.

"How do you think your time was here, overall?" Her pen is poised over a notebook, and she seems genuinely interested. It's weird to be seen when what you're dealing with is invisible.

I fold my knees like a child. "Really affirming. It's hard when you're stuck in your brain to know whether or not it's psychosomatic. Or if I'm making it up, like I can't believe it's real most of the time."

She gives a sad little smile. "It's not psychosomatic. Nor are you making it up. You're one of the worst of the worst cases we've had. It's very real."

This affirmation is the greatest gift the clinic gives me. It's the first time my disconnect from pain ties into reality. I finally understand what my journals reflect, and the shredded pieces of myself start to knit together, and I'm grounded. The affirmation gives me permission to stop erasing myself.

I've never before met so many people like me in one place. We have our own lingo, our own inside migraine jokes. We get it. I watch them suffer through the pain and see myself in all their tiny movements. Their faces twist, and my muscles twitch in the same way because the path is so well-worn.

Through the workshops, I realize I'm already doing everything I can. Quitting my job and trying to live within my limits was the best possible thing I could've done. It's why I'm not worse. Dear God, how could it possibly worse?

And because I'm doing everything I can, and I'm doing everything right, and this pain still isn't gone—it is real. This isn't fiction leaking into my real life. I'm not another character with made-up pain. I'm living nonfiction, in a sonnet that, despite all boundaries and rules, doesn't want to behave.

We talk about marriage and depression and the impact chronic illness has upon relationships. Randy chimes in with his questions and concerns. Having a professional who deals with hundreds of marriages like ours tell us that, yes, the boundaries we've set up in our relationships are good.

We've burned through almost all our time when I finally speak about the gnawing in my gut. "I do have one last question though."

The psychologist taps on her binder. "About marriage?"

"About writing." I look over to my backpack, to the laptop I had not opened except to watch *The Walking Dead*, with the book contract waiting for my signature and a list of edits that will take many, many hours to complete. "How do I keep creating?"

I know I'm grasping at sonnet rules again, trying to give my life shape and definition so I know how to live.

Her answer isn't helpful and makes me recoil inside.

"I'm sorry to say this, but you might not be able to."

46

Any self-help book dealing with pain and suffering will remind you that pain can't be controlled. We can't control when a migraine hits or when depression swings or when a car crashes. The books also say that the one thing you can control is your acceptance of the pain. I mentioned this before, because it's so important. It's part of any grief program, any counseling session, a staple that has proven to be true time and time again. If you only ever stay steeped in the anger and the "Why me?" question, you'll never find true joy or happiness despite the pain.

If you learn to accept the pain and embrace it, you can have a higher quality of life. I've experienced this phenomenon myself. If I simmer in anger, my quality of life diminishes. If I accept the pain, hold it close in a tender hug, peace does fill me for a time. I might not be the Disney Princess of Joy, but I am a bit happier.

The problem is that this advice makes acceptance sound

final. Like, have a kid and you'll forever be a parent. But acceptance, like forgiveness, isn't a one-time deal—which sucks, because I hate revisiting work.

I have to learn to accept and accept and accept again.

Yesterday, I could accept the pain. Today, checkout day, acceptance is a struggle.

The very idea of coming to peace with my pain makes my anger worse. I can sense it—a mini arctic shelf frozen over in my chest. It pushes against me, wanting to get out. Deep down, I think I'm a very angry person.

I want to say that peace is better than anger, except I don't think that's actually true. Righteous anger can be good, anger can be pure, anger can be right. I just have a hard time actually living out my belief. As much as the anger lives and breathes, I don't like the sensation.

But I also don't want to accept the pain. I don't want acceptance to be my only option. I want to transcend all this, I want to see new worlds, I want to do new things. I want my stars. I want my damn third option.

My chest responds, weighing even heavier and adding to my misery.

I wonder if the answer is to hold both emotions at once.

When I think about holding both anger and peace, I am more human. I mean, Jesus was both angry and at peace. He throws snappy comments at the religious leaders of his time. He flips over tables in the Temple to drive out the profiteers. He also plays with children. He takes time to chat with the outcasts by the well. To experience only one emotion is to simplify being human. We are far more complicated than to be colored by a single emotion. To categorize myself either as angry or as peaceful isn't honest. Anger and peace both burn bright by themselves; maybe holding them together I'll burn twice as bright.

So today I am angry. I am so, so, so very angry. Angry at my body, angry at my dreams, angry at God, angry at my pain, angry at living in general. I may have chosen some stupid things in my life, but I did not choose this.

I know I'll eventually be at peace again. I know I'll be okay. I know I'll be happy with the stories and lands stemming from my brain. I'll sense God's peace within me, a solid comfort and assurance. I'll find peace with my dreams, or, at least, a different version of my dreams. It'll be enough.

Just not right now.

47

Randy finishes my final paperwork, packs my suitcase and my nubby colored pencils, checks me out while I stare at the floor of my room. He gathers all the brochures and instructions for my follow-ups with my home neurologist, catalogues my new treatment plans and my new somewhat helpful abortives, and loads my suitcase into the car while I stare at the dashboard. If he tries to speak to me, I don't hear him. I am a husk.

He joins me in the car, piles all the go-home papers between us, and shuts the door. But he doesn't start the rental car.

There's only silence. A thick, heavy silence, of when you thought you reached the end of the chapter but find pages upon disheartening pages left. You're not at the end yet.

Silence.

And pain.

Always ever pain.

Randy puts his hand on my arm. His voice is thick and gentle. "It's okay, babe. It's okay to cry."

The tears come. Deep, soul-gutting sobs. Years and years of built-up emotion, of looking to the future and finding disappointment. Of finding hope and losing it through my fingers because it is as ethereal as starlight. The tears come so hard, surely I burst a blood vessel. My head shreds, but I can't stand using one of my new shot abortives, so I package the shreds and deal like I've been dealing all my life.

I don't feel any better.

In fact, I feel worse. Not because the clinic made the pain worse, but because I've spent so long without distraction I'm uncomfortably aware of how pain fills all corners of my life. I've spent two weeks paying attention to it. Two weeks letting it define my every movement. Two weeks letting it define every thought. I can suddenly see how clearly it colors every inch of my world.

Sure, I come away validated. I come away knowing I'm not alone, that there are others like me out there. I come away with a better understanding of the disconnect I've lived in my entire life. I come away knowing that I've done the best I can. But I was supposed to arrive at the clinic and find healing. I was supposed to come home to a new, magical life. Everything was supposed to change.

Instead, nothing did.

And I'm supposed to go back to my old life? Just like that? As though I'm not peering through the looking glass?

But there's nothing left to do but go home and wait to see if the vasospasm medicine works.

It is an anti-climax.

Randy stops at a Goodwill. He spends fifty bucks we can't afford on every gaudy porcelain dish set on the shelf and every stupid Precious Moments figurine. For a bonus, he even finds a sparkly unicorn snow globe. Turn it upside down and watch the magic rain.

He also buys a pickax.

"I'll just leave it at their house," he says as he loads it into the trunk. "It'll be a thank you gift for letting us stay." *Sure, babe, sure. Since everybody wants a pickax as a thank you.*

We drive to the forest right by our friend's place, where we will stay for three nights to give me some extra rest before flying home. Our car trunk rattles with all the china as we drive over the roots and logs. We open the hatchback and sit together with a permanent marker and write all my hopes, all my fears, all my wishes, all the stupid pithy phrases people say, all the reasons I hate God right then, all the ways I want to curl up and die already, all the things this disease has stolen from us, all of it all over those fancy porcelain plates and figurines.

I save the worst curse words for the unicorn snow globe.

We lay out this montage of blasphemy and frustration and anger and grief and honesty on a cheery blue picnic tarp. Another round of tears fill my eyes, but the act of writing stole whatever energy I had. Randy holds me as we both stare at our offering. He says a prayer and hands me the pickax. "Make sure to aim your swing."

I channel every inch of emotion from my heart through my arms, through my hands, and heave the pickax.

Together we smash our sacrifice.

48

I hoped this destructive act would drain me of my anger. It doesn't. I have so much anger that it has long since transformed into emptiness. In my imagination, I crush all those pretty porcelain pieces, and with each swing a tiny bit of me stitches together again, a tiny spark of hope flames to life. In reality, I have lost so much muscle I can barely lift the pickax.

And I'm so, *so* exhausted.

I destroy a single plate and the stupid unicorn snow globe.

I'm so empty, so broken, so not alive, Randy has to finish the smashing.

He even cleans up the entire mess without a single complaint, while I sit my empty self in the hatchback and listen for birdsong.

There is none.

49

Two months earlier:

Randy asks to borrow my painting supplies. I help him move my easel into his workshop space and pull out my woven basket of collected acrylics. He shuffles through my stacks of canvas, searching for the perfect size.

Then he shuts me out of the room.

After five hours, I fill a plate with taco leftovers and knock on the door. I open it with a slight creak.

He's sitting shirtless on a paint-speckled stool, red paint splattering his abdomen like blood. If I didn't know better, I would've thought he ripped out his heart. He clutches a paintbrush.

"Why?" His voice cracks. "Why is there so much suffering?"

The painting behind him is dark, like the hopeless night. Streaks of crimson, like whiplashes, scar lengthwise across the canvas. It reminds me of the scourging Jesus receives before being nailed to the cross.

I set down the plate and go to him.

Randy is a solid man, built more like a wrestler or a brick wall. About once a year, someone tries to recruit him into the police force or military. When he smiles, his face crinkles like a crepe and the day is eternally brighter. It's easy to look at him and think "unbreakable." That's not true. He's as breakable as anybody else.

He pulls me tight, sobbing into my hair. Paint smears onto my clothes.

"I'm so *furious*," he says through clenched teeth. "So furious it hurts."

I tighten my grip around him. "Me too."

We hold onto each other for a long, long time.

50

The garden is a boneyard. Picked over skeletons and concrete for miles. No sign of the roses and snapdragons that once filled the scenery. No sign of the pretty white iron rod fence. Dark clouds, the ominous type that speak of destruction, fill the sky, and nightmarish shadows creep out of the concrete cracks.

In the middle of this concrete jungle is Him.

His wrists are tied to a wooden whipping pole. His back is flayed, flesh hanging to expose muscle. The thorns make His skin a crown of ribbons. Purple, saffron yellow, and indigo bruises cover His face. His wrists are torn, and the gaping wound at His side pours water and scarlet.

Lightning slashes the sky. "Is it not enough?" His voice barely registers above a whisper. His ribs move when he speaks.

"No," I say. I tighten my grip on the whip. When did it appear in my hand? It, too, is crusted with blood. "I need you to feel what I feel," I say. "I don't need you to have your own pain. I need you to have my pain." I raise the whip.

He never breaks my gaze, only leans back to expose his spine to me. And gives a tiny nod.

I snap the whip, aiming for his temples.

His scream is beautiful.

It sounds so much like all the ones I want to scream, all the ones I silence because I don't want them to be heard. Lightning cracks open the sky again, the only sliver of light in this dark place. I bring the whip down again, pain for pain. I cry as I match each throb, match each spike, match each brain-numbing blow.

When my arms are numb, I drop the whip. My front is covered with gore, and my hands are stained crimson. "How is this not torture, what you let me go through?" My voice is raw, and my tongue tastes like blood that isn't mine. I stumble forward, draw my fist back, and punch Him. My knuckles split, and I wipe the blood onto my sweatshirt. I land another punch. Another. Until His eye is gone.

I fall to my knees. My jeans are soaked in His blood, and my muscles ache, and I hurt. The pain is still in my brain, and it won't go away. It won't go away. It never goes away. My tears taste salty and metallic and are thick like oil.

He lays there on his side, hands still tied to keep Him from falling completely over, face too swollen to blink, continuing to hold my gaze.

It only fuels the fire, fuels the pain. I yell at his body. "Why? *Why?*"

The only noise is the skeletons clattering in the wind.

His silence is like nails inside me. I shriek, launching to my feet. "Say something." I stand and kick Him, and a rib cracks. I do it again. Another bone breaks under my boot, but it feels good. Another kick. Another and another until His skull is as beat up as mine and his brain matter leaks onto the concrete. "What is the point of you?" My jaw is locked so tightly my voice hisses.

I try to kick Him again, but my legs won't move. They have sealed together. Scales dot where my jeans used to be. I've become a snake. My thick green body curls, and my scales rub in the blood. "What'ssss the point of you?" My tongue flicks. "Whatssss the point?"

Only now does He cry. Each teardrop restores a bit of His flesh. His hands become hands again. His ribs knit and heal to form a cage, then a chest, and his eye regenerates and takes on a rich hazel color.

My breathing heaves. I hate how He's healing. I hate how He won't stay down. I need Him to stay down.

He can lift His arms now. "Come here," He says.

I twist ,and my serpent's body morphs into child's legs. I toddle to Him through the gore. He reaches out and pulls me close until even my hair is bloodied and smells like copper.

"It's okay," He says. "It's okay."

We cry together until both of us are whole enough to do it all over again.

51

My favorite time of year is the calendar's last quarter. Bakersfield's four seasons are melt-your-makeup-hot, blistering hot, not quite as hot, and cool enough for grass to sprout. Imagine my surprise when I showed up to my Midwestern college and discovered *seasons* and *snow* and what sweater weather and UGG boots are really created for. It took me all of two days to realize my heart had been lost to October, November, and December. The *air* smells different this time of year, all crisp and snappy and cinnamon. I'll gladly trade all my summer months for any spare Octobers.

However, my favorite holiday is in the spring: Good Friday.

Ash Wednesday starts Lent, and we mark our foreheads with ash. An early morning service and a massive gut-stretching brunch marks Easter. But we rarely pause to mark Good Friday. Even if there's a service, most of the time it's a disappointment. It's quiet, silent, painful, but with no forehead ashes to help with the remembering.

Without Good Friday, without the day Jesus was beaten, bloodied, broken, Lent and Easter wouldn't exist.

Several books tell me being crucified is the worst possible way to die. To gain understanding, all you have to do is keep your nausea under control and watch a movie like *The Passion of the Christ*. I've been told that Jesus died through crucifixion *because* it's the worst way to die. I've been told that Jesus can understand your pain because He's been through the worst pain possible.

Maybe that's right. Maybe people who are way smarter than me, who are way more educated than me, got together and agreed this is technically correct.

Personally, this isn't good enough.

I'm fully aware of how arrogant this sounds. That I, one single human in the speck of all of history, can think Christ's suffering wasn't enough. Who am I to *think* such a thing, let alone to write it?

But—I'd be lying if I said otherwise. Christ in pain *isn't* good enough.

When I'm in pain, I don't care that Christ was pierced by a spear. When my brain feels full of blood, I don't care that Christ was beaten raw. If I'm really being honest, I want to scream, *His pain didn't last more than three days! Mine is worse!*

Here's where you're really going to hate me—He *died.* How many of us have pain that *cannot kill*? That seems like so much worse of a sentence, to be stuck with the promise that the pain won't end unless you end first. How can Christ possibly understand that? If I'm really going for the gold honesty ribbon, I'll admit that I don't trust that Christ can understand my pain unless He suffered *even more* pain than me. And truth be told, one to three days doesn't cut it. For some of us, fifteen years hanging on that cross wouldn't be enough.

I have this idea.

Let's assume you all agree with me and believe God exists outside the construct of time. He can enter and exit time at will and is more than past, present, future. He can visit all the Octobers and Novembers and Decembers because He is *in* all the Octobers and Novembers and Decembers. All of them, all at once, always.

Maybe that moment on the cross is infinite. An eternal moment.

It exists as a constant in all of time. Because God lives in all the Octobers and Novembers and Decembers, Christ can *still* be on the cross, even now, in pain.

Maybe, in that eternal moment, He's not just experiencing His pain. He's experiencing *my* pain. All my pain, everything I've felt, everything I will feel, all at once. Then, in that eternal moment, He's experiencing all *your* pain. Everything you've felt, everything you will feel, all at once.

Not being bound by time, He could relive every person's pain, feel every broken heart, experience every brain malfunction. Maybe He went through *exactly* what I have felt and what I will feel.

This is what I want from God—to know He feels *my*

pain. To know He understands *exactly* what I've been through. Every heartache, every migraine, every random stabbing in my stomach, every aura that never seems to end, because He went through it too. And then He suffered His own pain on top of it.

I have no idea if this is theologically correct, but it feels right. When my body is splitting and I feel like I should be dying, and Easter feels a lifetime away, that's what I need to know. That Christ still lives in an eternal moment of pain that's infinitely bigger than anything I can experience. He knows.

It's a sliver I cling to.

52

We fly home. Apollo and Athena lick my face, and I sweep my arms around them in a bear hug. Randy dumps my suitcase over the washer and begins laundry. My parents and aunt and uncle have filled our fridge with easy meals and frozen soups, our pantry with quick snacks. The house is shining clean, and a bouquet of sunny welcome-home flowers graces our living room.

I pet the pups while Randy pops a frozen pizza into the oven and sit in my navy chair, stained with paint flecks flung from my art loft above, and wait.

I don't know why I sign the book contract. Honestly, putting that pressure on myself is a stupid thing to do. I'm still so used to *going* I don't know how to say no to an opportunity. If I had the chance again, I wouldn't sign. But I'm also glad I didn't know better and signed. I send off the contract and am immediately torn between regret and a shadow of pleasure. The book will eventually be published, but today it is a mess on my hard drive. I have time before I need to turn in revisions, so I set aside the laptop and smell the cooking pizza.

The next day I wake, do some revisions, and sit in the chair.

The next day I wake, do some revisions, and sit in the chair.

The next day I wake, do some revisions, and sit in the chair.

And the next.

And the next.

And the next.

I do not pray. I do not read. I do not paint.

I do the bare minimum required, because my gears are broken and I'm stuck in a clockwork ghost world, and I sit.

I sit.

I sit in that chair, empty and broken and hollow, oh so hollow, for months.

POSTDROME

After the pain phase ends, the migraine still isn't done. Your body enters a hangover stage filled with its own special symptoms. This can last as long as the attack itself. I've given my entire self over to the pain, and I have nothing left to give. I tell myself, *I did it. I made it through.* And I wait for this heavy, empty stage to fade.

After finishing a creative project, I have nothing left to give. I've poured my entire self into the work and am hollow. But I'm not ready to start something new. Not yet. The idea of again seems too big. Instead, I savor the moment—*I did it. I made it through.* And I wait for the empty stage to fade.

Genesis 2:1-2a

"Thus the heavens and the earth, and all the host of them were finished. And on the seventh day God ended His work which He had completed, and He rested."

53

There are a couple ideas about pain and suffering spouted as platitudes in Christian culture. For some reason, I've heard these platitudes more often on the more conservative side of Christianity. I'm not sure why. I've even been told this to my face before: God gave me migraines to teach me a lesson.

The saying implies that once I learned my lesson, my pain will be gone. Therefore, since I'm still in pain every single day, I have not learned my lesson. Whoever tells me this always wears a mask of sympathy, as though they pity all the soul work I better hurry up and do if I want to escape the pain.

I really, really hate this idea, because it also implies I'm not listening to God and am just plain stubborn in my self-destructive ways. Profound stubbornness is written in my DNA, so, yes, I am stubborn, but I'm not stupid. If an area of my life needs to change, I'll change.

I lump the saying in with the idea of, "God's trying to

teach me not to sin." It's the story of the blind man Jesus heals in the book of John. It goes something like this:

> Disciple 1: Hey, look, man. Blind
> dude at 3 o'clock!
> Disciple 2: Sucks to be him. Doesn't
> he know if he confessed his sin,
> he could see again?
> Disciple 1: Yeah. His blindness is his
> fault. He needs to learn his lesson.
> Jesus, overhearing: That's the
> stupidest idea I've ever heard.
> Disciples 1 and 2: *blinks*

Then Jesus gives another reason of why the man might be blind, and it has nothing to do with learning a lesson.

The other statement I hear a lot is, "God gave you migraines so you could bless somebody else." Often they mean this as, "God gave you migraines so you can teach other people what you learned."

It's a good thought. To be honest, for the first six years of being chronic, I leaned on this to find some purpose. The problem with the saying is that it implies my pain isn't valid unless it's for the purpose of somebody else. My pain cannot exist by itself. All my suffering, all my loss, is for somebody else's gain. I become the scapegoat for somebody else's life lesson. Its strips away my autonomy and sense of self. I cannot own my own suffering.

I do think God sometimes uses the consequences of our choices to teach us a lesson. AKA: The consequence of heavy-use, long-term smoking is lung cancer. But I don't think "lesson learning" is the primary reason we have pain.

There is a term for it in the medical field. Migraines are my "primary diagnosis." They are not a symptom of another problem. For me, migraine is a root problem that exists by itself. For somebody with a primary diagnosis of fibromyalgia, migraines might be a symptom of fibromyalgia, not the root. Anyone who has spent time in a doctor's office can tell you treating only symptoms won't get rid of the root problem. It can help, but symptom chasing doesn't make any true permanent change.

Yes, I do think God can use my experience to help other people. I think He often does. I've seen it. One of the reasons I'm bothering to write all this is because someone out there needs to know they aren't alone. In this way, my words can help others. But again, back to that primary versus symptom idea: God does not give me pain for the primary purpose of blessing other people. God does not devalue me for somebody else's gain. You never once see that in the Bible. Jesus always adds value to people.

I think pain just happens. We live in a shitty, broken world. Pain is the natural consequence of living in it.

Back to the blind man. The Pharisees are in a tizzy, because how *dare* Jesus value a person more than following the *no healing* on the sabbath rules. They drag the newly seeing man into the Temple and put him on trial.

"How were you healed? How did this happen? When, why, who, what, how?"

They even bring in his parents.

Eventually the man verbally throws up his hands. "Look. I can't answer all this. I don't know the mechanics of miracle-working. I don't even know what the guy looks like. Remember? Blind? But this is what I do know. I was blind. Now I see."

I can't solve the problem of pain. I can't even give you a why. But I do know this: God loves me. God is in pain with me. And someday, someday the root problem will be fixed, the broken world repaired, and the pain will be gone.

54

Sometimes I am two people.

The first Abby is excited and happy about life. She's the person who plops in the restaurant seat in a flouncy-bouncy dress across from her handsome husband on the first date they've had in a while. Close by is a mile-long walking path that borders a lake by Barnes and Noble. Her favorite thing is to eat shrimp, walk along the path, stop for a book, and end the whole evening with some frozen yogurt. Adrenaline bubbles inside her as they dream of places to travel, new jobs, new teaching and painting opportunities, even adding to the potential kid-name list, despite recently being warned by doctors that this isn't the best idea. This Abby lives with childlike wonder.

The second Abby isn't so lucky. She sits in the same chair, across from the same handsome husband who's enjoying tacos, but a sob hovers at the back of her throat. Under the soft fluorescent light, surrounded by food smells, the temperature outside slightly too hot for comfort, her fingers keep grasping for the glass of Diet Coke. The shot she took the day before to squash the migraine isn't working. The caffeine keeps the edge off the pain long enough for her to keep that sob stifled. She pictures rolling up her brain, folding all the pain and squishing it like a pancake into a size her body can control and ignore. But the throbbing resists and crawls out of mental reach like a cockroach. All she wants to do is go home, hide in the dark, cover her misbehaving brain with a blanket, and let the sob out. This Abby has lived with too much pain.

It's been six months since the clinic, and I've been hiding in the dark for the last week. Three days completely lost to migraine. Two with a couple hours of writing. The one thirty-minute walk I took resulted in the migraine that would not calm even with a shot. I miss the sunshine. I miss the fresh air. I miss leaving my house. So I split myself in two and let Abby #1 out for a couple hours while Abby #2 keeps the body functioning so I can go on a date with my husband. I'm counting the months until the new medications are on the market.

I hate living with these two sides of myself.

How do you be present and authentic in relationships when, just to show up, you have to ignore half of yourself? How can you give your entire self to somebody when you can't even stitch your two selves together?

In these moments, I don't know which Abby is more true. Or maybe both Abbys are entirely true. Maybe it's a paradox.

Most true things in life seem to be.

My life is worth both a dust speck in the span of the universe and also the life of the infinite God. I am one person but also two—combined in a marriage vow. Creating art means both to be its master and its servant. Christ is both one hundred percent God and one hundred percent human. My writing work is both worth fighting for and totally disposable. To love others means both to fight for them and to leave them to their choices.

I am both in pain and not in pain.

Both are completely true.

55

After a nearly a year, my vasospasm treatment begins to work, and I'm doing a little better. I'm not curled on the couch for as long each day, and it makes a big difference for my mental health. We decide now is a good time to focus on Randy's career. He has switched from pastoral work to construction. While he enjoys working with his hands, and is good at it, my ongoing medical bills say this is not a permanent solution. I sign him up for a LifePlanning course to help him find what he's passionate about, what he's skilled at, and what potential job could combine these two as well as meet our financial needs.

Waiting for job application responses is strangely like querying a novel. A query is the introduction letter sent to an agent or editor to see if your book is a good fit for them or the publishing house. It's usually the first step to getting traditionally published. You throw a part of yourself into the void and can only refresh your email so many times without going crazy. Randy sends out several, including one to build stages for a local high school. I can easily picture him building friendships with the students. He hovers over his phone waiting for the callbacks.

While we wait, we visit his family for Christmas. The previous two winters, I canceled our visit due to those multi-attacks. Instead of Christmas cookies, I devoured steroids. Ho ho ho, happy holidays.

I stand next to the aisle after the service at Randy's childhood church trying to remember the names of my in-laws' friends. Thanks to the brain fog, the only way I can remember names is due to the slight muscle memory of handwriting all those wedding invitations so long ago. I can't remember the person, but I remember writing their name in flawless font. I don't like making others feel irrelevant, as though I can't be bothered to retain their name, so I don't tend to approach people I should know because of this.

One woman nears me. I can't remember her name or her connection to the family to save Apollo's life. "How are your headaches?" she asks.

Considering travel does a number on my body, it's kind of her to ask. The fact she knows about the migraines says my in-laws have been filling her in on all my medical stuff. I love when they do this, because it means I never have to. And it means my answers can be more honest since they already know my backstory.

I lean back on my heels. "Actually, I had a bit of progress and a setback this year. But we're working on it. I've been doing a lot of work learning contentment in that this is a lifelong—"

"Don't say that." Her words are clipped, and she folds her arms.

I blink. "What?"

"Don't say that this is lifelong. We don't know the future."

All my goodwill toward her dies.

Insert rapid internal monologue: *Well, of course we don't know the future, nobody knows the future. But I know you're saying this because you think God will heal me, but it's been ten years and so far He hasn't and I've had so many more conversations with Him about this than you and I've never gotten the sense that He is going to heal me and don't you dare recommend going to healing prayer because I'm sick of having palms laid on me and hearing fervent words whispered and seeing hopes crushed and I STILL am not healed and what about Paul anyway who prayed three times and if God didn't heal him, then why should I think that I deserve being healed so this is going to be an irrelevant conversation.*

All that in about three seconds.

Something must show on my face, because she steps back. *Thanks for the betrayal, body.* That's the biggest drawback about life sans Botox. Not all the tiny lines appearing in my forehead now that I'm creeping closer to being middle-aged. Not all the tiny twitches as my dead muscles try to rebuild. But the fact that people can read my micro-expressions again. It sucks.

She backtracks, speaking over her shoulder as she scuttles sideways out of my way. "There's always advances in science for migraine and new developments. And I saw this new treatment on Facebook the other day—"

"Yes, I'm aware. My doctor is on top of all the new treatments." I sound ruder than I mean to be.

But the woman is gone. As if my answer doesn't matter because it isn't the right one.

This frustrates me.

I love the Church. I love the Church body. But if anything's been made clear to me, it's that the Church doesn't know how to handle illness or artists. We want to fix, to heal, and then move on. We want to say our prayers and see an immediate result. We don't know how to sit in the pain, be okay, and not have answers.

I think that's why artists haven't felt welcome in the Church for a long time. Art is messy. The process is rarely linear and is filled with questions and doubts and wrestling and not having answers. As followers of Christ, we're supposed to enter into the messy.

Echoing writer and poet Kathleen Norris, Christianity is a blood religion. Our very doctrine is based in blood. And blood is messy.

Churches should be the first to fling open their doors and welcome the mess. But so often we don't. And when we shut our doors to keep the insides neat and tidy, not only do we lock out mystery and wonder and awe, but we also lock out all the wonderful things those in pain and artists have to teach us.

56

Pain separates what you think you believe from what you actually believe. It's about as pleasant as Aslan stripping away Eustace's dragon skin in *The Voyage of the Dawn Treader*. When the scales are gone, you're forced to face what lies underneath. Sometimes what's left doesn't look remotely human. It's an awful truth.

I think that's why a lot of churches are so willing to dole out unhelpful phrases like, *Ask and you will receive*, and, *Spend more time reading the Bible*, or, *Pain is God's way of getting our attention*, like mini Snickers bars on Halloween. They are comforting phrases and draw easy boundaries for pain. If your circumstances violate these boundaries, then clearly the problem is with you—not the drawn boundaries.

But when your body and your thoughts are fighting you —when the very nature of what you deal with pushes boundaries—what then?

You have to start asking harder questions. You have to go deeper. What do you truly believe about life? Do you believe life is worth struggling through? Is your life valuable even if spent in pain? Do you believe in something, anything substantial? Do you believe God is in pain with you? Do you believe He doesn't care? Is this hill of pat phrases one you're willing to be buried on? Or is there a richer hill just beyond your sight, but getting there requires some hiking?

I want you to wrestle with the questions. I want you to put away your phrase book and your quotes and face what's underneath all the scales. Face *why* you're so content to draw boundaries. Face your discomfort. Face your own ugly truth and your own pain. Because maybe you're more scared about erasing the safety walls you've built around your life. Without your hand-drawn boundaries, you might have to make some harder decisions. Without your hand-drawn boundaries, you might have to reevaluate the box you put God in. Without your hand-drawn boundaries, you might realize you live in a much vaster, much messier, much more chaotic, much more beautiful and magical world than you thought.

Maybe, eventually, you'll look around and realize there are greener hills to lay your headstone on. Maybe your quote book wasn't all that important anyway.

Ask the questions.

Then come sit with me.

Please.

I want you to come sit with me.

I want you to get me a new ice pack, fill my needles with my abortive medicine, lace your fingers through mine, and be willing to have your hand broken in my vice-like grip.

That speaks love to me more than quoting words ever will.

57

When Christ died, the veil was torn. Though I'm not convinced the veil was torn completely open. We only receive glimpses of the other side. Of eternal life, of spirit-things, of other. Some days, when I'm alone or surrounded by people, I feel as though I can reach out and touch the other side because the veil is slightly thinner in this spot in time and space. The sensation only confirms I have yet to step through the veil. I may be home, but I'm not *home* yet.

No matter what happens during my life, I still have to step through the veil. Knowing the greatest wonder is yet to come, that the pain has not drained everything, that there's still a bit of magic left, is a great comfort.

58

In stories, there is a magical turning moment. The point where the hero learns what they need to overcome their obstacle. A dawning of understanding. They are metaphorically killed and come back to life just in time to beat the villain. They've passed the trial. They won. They return home victorious.

In Sarah J. Maas' *Heir of Fire*, a scene near the end depicts the main character in a metaphorical pit. She's lost everything: friends and family and the will to live. The people she failed line up and whip her. She embraces the punishment. She's so empty she wants to die. But she can't.

Like a ghost, her past self appears, a child, and holds out her hand. *Get up*, her past self whispers. *Get up*.

Get up. Get up. Get up.

The main character rises and explodes into flames, burning away the enemy. She wins the battle, saving countless lives in the process.

I don't have a moment like that.

I don't have a moment where my heart begins beating again. I can't point to a paintbrush or a plot point or a piece of liturgy or an image of my past self and say, *This is it. This is what helped.* Maybe all of it, maybe none of it, maybe a mix. Maybe the act of creating part of another book triggers my heartbeat because it's the closest thing to prayer I can manage, the pure joy of making something new. Who knows.

My heart just begins beating.

A beat here. A week passes and another beat there. Two weeks later and there's three beats, *Wagoosh wagoosh wagoosh.* Backward, no beats at all for a while. Forward, another beat.

Until a year passes, and my heart beats regularly again. Weak, but the pulse is present.

I'm home, and I'm not victorious. The villain isn't defeated.

But I'm alive.

I'm alive, and perhaps with enough time I'll build enough strength to get up. It won't be today. It probably won't be tomorrow. But maybe the next day.

Or the next.

Or the next.

59

I knew my first published book was different as soon as I wrote the practice page. An idea can spend a year or more percolating in the junk end of my thoughts until it is strong enough to bring to the forefront. Before I even begin writing the book, I'll create a couple pages of practice writing, just to make sure the voice clicks. Kind of like checking a simmering stew of creativity. If the voice isn't there, then the story stew isn't ready. Within two paragraphs of my practice page, I fall in love with my main character's voice.

But I also fall in love with one of the series' themes. The loss and cost of dreams. Is a dream worth the sacrifice?

We are told, Yes! Yes! Dreams are always worth it. Any sacrifice, all the sacrifice. Especially here in America. This country runs on dreams. Look at the musical *Hamilton*, which I both love and hate.

I wince when I say that aloud because I fear I'll be executed by every creative person ever. I love the music, I love the story, and who doesn't fall in love with that drinking scene—the genius group of friends deciding to be *more.*

We use, *I'm not going to throw away my shot*, and, *The plan is to fan this spark into a flame*, and, *The room where it happens* as our creative anthems. Our rallying cry to give 110 percent and to create our Dream. We print phrases on T-shirts and stickers and hang them as inspirational posters above our creative workplaces. Those are great, well-written rallying cries, and they make my heart tremble with possibility.

But we also use them as anthems to justify destruction.

An affair? Well, if it supports our Dream. A marriage completely falling apart? Well, if it supports our Dream. A damaged relationship with a child? Well, if it supports our Dream.

Marriages, families, relationships—all of it can be sacrificed on the altar of our Dream.

That's what I disagree with.

Our Dream should not trump people. It should not trump personhood. Our Dream is just that—a dream. If you haven't read *Big Magic* by Elizabeth Gilbert, you should. It's basically an entire book about how creativity is marvelous, magical, and frivolous. A dream, not a Dream.

I get through college, at the expense of being couch-ridden for years. I eventually publish my book, again at the expense of my body, and recovery takes far longer than I plan. I have to back off the minimal amount of marketing to a negligible amount. I have to spread my deadlines even farther apart. I can't keep pursuing this at the cost of my body.

I'm still learning how to live like a sonnet.

How can you tell the difference between a dream worth the sacrifice and one that isn't? What if our sacrifice negatively impacts other people? What if it negatively impacts *ourselves*? Do we even have the right to make such a decision?

Culture says yes.

I'm not so sure.

60

Few things make me more furious than knowing I'm only giving 70 percent. Right now, as I write this, I'm working on the sequel to my first published book. I have a list of scenes pinned to my whiteboard, a list of edits that need to be done to those scenes, and a countdown of two weeks before I hand over the pages.

My heart chugs, and I want to bust out all the changes so I can spend the last two weeks actually making this manuscript readable. I want to finish smoothing out the scratches so I can put on a finishing coat. For me, this means tugging character arcs and massaging voices so all the characters don't sound like they have the same conscience.

But it hurts.

The questions flood me: How do I write? How do I create? How much do I lean into the pain? When do I choose to live despite the pain? When do I choose to step aside and let the pain run its course because living will make it worse? Where's the line? Where's the bloody handbook?

It's a year and a half after the clinic, and I *still* wrestle with these questions.

I have so much guilt when I'm not working. Like an iron ribbon threading through my core. I think this guilt is because Americans value hard work. No, that isn't right, we find our identity in hard work. No, not even that. We find our identity in overworking and pushing ourselves too far. It's part of the American Dream. If we work hard enough, go far enough, dream big enough, we can achieve anything. The idea that we have to stop before we've hit our limit, that we need to stop before we push ourselves too far—that we might not achieve everything we want—it's sacrilege.

I'm not even in the corporate world, but I sense the pressure every time I don't pull out the laptop. For writing, you are told to find the best story. Even if finding the best story takes you through multiple nights and several extra rounds of revisions and brings you to the brink of sanity. Even if finding the best story means you now have a major case of anxiety any time you sit to scribble. Give, not 100 percent, but 110 percent.

All for the sake of the story, all for the sake of the best version of art.

We don't have "good enough" in our vocabulary.

We don't know how to make good enough art.

I've been learning to make "good enough" art. To call a painting finished because my pain says it's finished rather than when I have completed all the details I have yet to fix.

Quitting early keeps me from overpainting anyway. To call this plot point "good enough" because I've spent enough time on making it original and my pain won't let me keep brainstorming options if I'm going to meet that deadline.

In learning how to make "good enough" art, I'm learning how to live a "good enough" life.

I don't need to aggravate my pain and speed clean to have my house together for guests. I just need to provide space for us to have a beer and a set of clean sheets for the bed. I don't need to make a perfect meal, just one that fills the belly. I don't need to have the perfect phrase to say when somebody confides in me. I just need to listen. I don't need to have every single one of my dreams fulfilled. I just need to learn how to be content.

But in living a "good enough" life, I find that, in a way, my dreams are fulfilled. I'm happier and more joyful. I'm truly enjoying the process of creating. Writing stories and creating music and painting canvas is lifegiving. And, for some magical reason, my pain tends to work more symbiotically with my art. I don't have to push myself as much, which I always had to do before, to find joy and complete my art.

I am enjoying my "good enough" life. I love my husband. I love my dogs. I love my house. I love the time I can spend creating, even if I have to schedule around the pain.

It's not what I want, but I am content giving my 70 percent.

I am not physically healed. But, in a way, I find emotional healing.

That's why I love the word *valiant*. The definition I

relate to most says the word originated in France during the fourteenth century. This definition says: *To the soldiers fighting, who gave all they had in the moment—even if it was not all they were capable of.*

I like that. The definition reframes what giving 100 percent means. My 70 percent is truly 100 percent, because it's 100 percent of what I can give to my dreams without sacrificing my personhood, my marriage, my family, my relationships.

I'm capable of more. But this is all I have to give.

It is valiant. It is enough.

Does this mean I have found my own version of the American Dream?

61

Managing migraine is about as easy as juggling balls created by a supervillain. You can keep a couple balls in the air, then BAM, one develops a sharp edge and you get cut. You lose control of the balls and it's pockets full of posey as they come tumbling down. But because you juggled so quickly and all the balls fell at the same time, you can never be one hundred percent sure which one did the damage. On the ground, the balls all look normal.

Then you realize, *This game is rigged. All* the balls might cut.

If every ball is a potential culprit, do you give up juggling? But what if your life calling is to juggle?

Or, worse, what if you hate juggling but are stuck in the circus called life and are obligated as a human being to juggle?

How does anyone answer these questions?

Even this week, still at my in-laws, I have five potential balls, and one or all could be carrying the sharp edge.

One: I'm trying to do some brainstorming work for a new book. Thinking and migraine take up the same head space, so my body is exhausted trying to play peacemaker between the two cohabiters.

Two: Traveling. The stress on my body usually does a number on me. I try to be extremely picky about traveling. If I drop this ball completely, I will never see my in-laws. Randy could visit his family by himself . . . But I enjoy spending time with them too.

Three: This ball has two bulges on it: lack of sleep and a bunch of new medicine. Any one of the bulges could carry the sharp edge.

Four: There's a massive storm outside, and weather is a notorious trigger for migraine.

Five: We're still trying to figure out a new job for Randy, and the process is stressful. Not only did the stage job fall through, but so did Plans B through F. He's trying to keep himself busy by filling out more job applications, journaling about life, and knocking out house to-do's for his parents.

Five massive balls that I can name off the top of my head that could be impacting me.

Juggle. Juggle. Juggle.

Which one has the edge today?

62

Vermont is *frigid*. Snow crackles beneath my feet as I crunch toward the auditorium. My snow coat is buckled tight around me, and my hands are stuffed into the thickest gloves I own. My breath makes ghost clouds in the night. Only for Anna's graduation ceremony from her MFA program will I risk hypothermia. My body is empty and weary from visiting Randy's family last week, but this is a trip I don't want to miss.

Randy holds out a swathed hand to help me walk across the ice. My old snow boots sink almost to my calves.

Each of the graduates read from a finished manuscript and have professors speak words over them before receiving their degree. Anna's new husband, Rob, wraps his arms around her. He's extremely tall, bone-thin, and loves her deeply. She clutches her finished printed manuscript while she waits her turn.

Anna's green dress brings out her eyes when she strides

onto the stage. She flips to a selected passage and reads a section from her manuscript aloud. Her voice is resonant, but she still isn't truly herself. She's still a shadow. You can tell by the way she barely interacted with any of her professors during the appetizers. She accepts her degree to cheers and sits, still grasping onto her husband and book like the lifelines they are.

When I smile at her, she doesn't respond, only looking past me toward an oncoming storm only she can see. I can't tell how much of her reaction is bipolar disorder and how much is our relationship still mending. I ignore her response, tucking away the sting so it doesn't hurt, and grin larger anyway. At least she's here and present. At least she finished her program.

At least her heart has begun beating again.

63

If you run in Christian circles for long, you'll hear the metaphor of the potter and the clay. Part of me wonders if the Bible uses this imagery because it was the most common art form of the time, so more people could relate.

The new medication the clinic doctors told me about is announced. It's called monoclonal antibodies or CGRP antibodies. It works by attaching to CGRP protein receptors in the brain to keep the proteins from docking. It's a new class of medicine and supposed to be a wonder drug for those who've failed out of other medications. Like me. In the trials, some were completely pain-free. Others found an overall fifty percent reduction in their migraines. Most found a measure of improvement.

What exact role does CGRP have in migraine? Yeah. Add that to the list of Things Scientists Don't Know.

Meanwhile, my aunt invites an artist to set up shop in her basement and teach a group of us about pottery. As I sit cross-legged in the audience listening to her drop metaphor after metaphor about pottery, it almost seems like the art sprung from the metaphor. Not the other way around.

It takes an absurd amount of strength and accuracy to center your lump of clay in the wheel. Without centering, as the wheel begins to turn, the lump of clay will wobble and, if you're like me, fly off the wheel completely and splatter on the cabinets.

The clay is also hard to move. I used to be more muscular, before pain took away most of my ability to exercise. When I first touched clay six years ago, the clay was stiff but movable. This time, the clay is impossible to move.

After a while, the clay warms and eventually I can push the cool squishy lump with less difficulty. I center the clay and spin the wheel, my arms and legs shaking to keep the mass from sliding around. More often than not, the clay has mastery over me.

Those in Christian circles often say this is how God uses suffering. If not centered on Christ first, then when suffering/pressure comes, our lumpy life becomes off-balance and we go spinning spinning spinning out of control. More musculature and strength and pain are needed to get us centered again.

But then, after warmth and softening, not as much suffering/pressure is needed. A slight touch will create a lip. A wet finger will create a design.

Through suffering/pressure, we are shaped into something beautiful.

I hate this metaphor.

Every fiber of my body rebels against the idea that suffering is needed to shape us, especially in the beginning, when we have so far to go.

Then there's clay grit. Apparently, different clay can withstand different temperatures. Butter-smooth porcelain is breathtakingly beautiful when fired but cannot be exposed to higher heat. It will break.

Other clay, the grittier and rougher kind, is not nearly as breathtaking when finished. But if you're going to use high heat, you want that type. The grit allows the clay to withstand soaring temperatures.

I've seen people break under a fraction of the pain I've experienced. I've seen people withstand three times the amount of pain I've been through. I've seen people who have never broken. Perhaps the difference depends on whether or not we are the type of clay that can withstand differing types of temperatures.

I come from a family of strong women. A family of stubborn, loud, determined women. In a culture that admires quieter, more compliant females, we stick out. We are the awkward grit that rubs palms raw. You could say that women like us, women with higher grit, are the women who can withstand the most searing fires.

Maybe my circumstances were always going to lead to this pain. Maybe God shaped my personality and my family genetics to ensure I had the grit to survive this fire. Maybe not.

Reminds me of a sermon I once heard, a new take on the disciple Peter walking on water.

This story is always told through the lens of failure: Peter saw Jesus, got out of the boat, and walked on water. Then when he saw waves, he lost faith, and sank.

Cause, meet Effect.

He lacked faith, he lost his center, and he sank.

But let's flip this idea upside down. As a pastor once pointed out, perhaps sinking was always part of the plan. Maybe Peter didn't sink because he lost faith. Maybe Peter's lack of faith was due to his sinking. Pain and suffering is just part of the bigger picture, part of the bigger story.

That's a metaphor I do resonate with.

64

One of my favorite things about our house is my bathtub. In our apartment, Randy would keep the water hot by boiling a tea kettle and topping off the water every fifteen minutes. The water never reached higher than my belly button. Now it can reach my collarbone if I fold my legs.

I fill the water and toss in a bath bomb, a gift from my mom. Lavender reaches my nose, and I inhale the lovely scent and pull out a book about body positivity. I made tons of body image progress in college and thought I didn't have any more work to do. But I realize now how much I hate my body for being in pain.

For so long, I've investigated my body, interrogated it like a suspect. Even the language I use divides me against my body, me against my head. I run my hand along my thighs and pull my knees to my chest and give myself a hug. My body has carried me through this illness. It has endured shots and floods of medication. It has built scar tissue to protect itself. It has carried emotional and physical weight it was never intended to bear. But it keeps getting up. It keeps going, even when I don't want it to.

All these years, my body hasn't been trying to work against me but *with* me. It doesn't want to hide secrets but help me discover them. My body wants to be friends.

It *is* my friend.

I watch the distortion of my legs underneath the still-fizzing bath bomb.

I picture an era before time begins, when God lays out all the possible bodies for my soul to inhabit. My soul studies each one before settling on the one currently soaking in the bath.

This one, it whispers. *This one can handle what will be asked of it.*

65

The pastor at my church speaks about the miracle of Lazarus. In short: Lazarus was sick, his sisters sent word to Jesus, and Jesus did not go "because he loved them." Even though he had the power to heal Lazarus. It seems completely counterintuitive. If Jesus loved his friend, wouldn't he want to save him?

Then Lazarus died. Only then did Jesus arrive, did Jesus speak. Then, in another biblical plot twist: Lazarus rose from the dead.

The pastor uses the passage to show one of the reasons behind suffering. We suffer so that God can show us His glory, because He loves us so much He would not want us to miss out on the miracle. I do think this can happen. Obviously, it did with Lazarus.

But I wrinkle my nose when people point to this story as the path God uses for my pain, and, if I'm really being honest, for others. It sounds sadistic.

What's tricky about this particular miracle is that the suffering in question didn't belong to Lazarus.

The suffering was for his sisters, Mary and Martha, who had to grieve their brother's premature death.

In fact, Lazarus didn't seem to suffer much at all. Sure, he was sick. But remember: Jesus spent a little over three years doing ministry. The other times he encountered Mary and Martha, nothing was said about Lazarus being sick. With the lack of scientific knowledge back then, he probably got taken out by a cold or something mundane that today we can pop a pill for. Or even if his illness was more serious, we can assume he didn't suffer for a very long time before he died.

The thing about being dead is: Once you're dead, you're dead. You're no longer in pain.

To me, that's the first fundamental difference between Lazarus's story and mine. My migraines haven't stopped.

The second biggest difference between the Lazarus story and other healing stories in the Bible and mine is that there was a clear turning point. A man blind, next moment he can see. A man paralyzed, next moment he can walk. A man dead, next moment he's alive.

Perhaps I just haven't had my turning point yet.

Is it fair to live in the "yet"?

How much of living in the "yet" means living in hope? How much of living in the "yet" means not accepting your reality? How much am I allowed to live for the day I can receive the CGRP antibodies? How much of my life can I pin on this hope?

I don't want to hit my twelve-year mark and be crushed because I was expecting a turning point miracle. I also don't want to live in denial.

Living with chronic illness means learning how to hold onto both reality and hope. I am sick. This is reality. I am not healed, yet. This is hope.

Again, there can be truth in both.

66

I'm bored of my routine of sitting, painting, and writing, so I drive the fifteen minutes to my parents' home. I perch at the kitchen counter with a cup of mocha in one hand. Three-fourths hot chocolate, three pumps of vanilla syrup, a good splash of almond milk. I like my coffee to not taste like coffee. Trapped behind the dog gate in the mudroom, Apollo and Athena whine. They look at me with comically huge eyes, begging to be let out where the people are.

I watch my mom dice onions for dinner. She's wearing a workout outfit in hopes of going on a walk that will probably not happen. I'm staying for dinner, since Randy is working late and driving over here drained any energy I have for making food. She wipes away tears with the back of her hand and walks away from the onion so she can breathe. She looks at my giant dogs with pursed lips.

"Have you ever considered getting smaller dogs?" She approaches the onion again, butcher knife in hand.

I roll my eyes. We've had this conversation many times. As much as my family claims to like dogs, they only like tiny dogs, ones that are ten pounds or less. And mine are six times that size. "No," I say. "Besides, when we got Apollo, I wanted a dog big enough to wrap my arms around to help anchor me through the suicide thoughts."

Her knife freezes mid-slice. "Suicide thoughts? What do you mean suicide thoughts?"

I swirl the dredges of my coffee-non-coffee. "Oh, you know, cause the pain can be so bad."

"The pain is that bad?"

I look at her. At the knife wavering in her hand. Didn't she know this? It wasn't like my pain is a secret. "Yeah, I mean. Why do you think I went to counseling all those years?"

She blinks back tears. I can't tell if it's from the onion or not. "I didn't know that's why you bought Apollo."

"Didn't I tell—"

"You never used the word 'suicide' before." She sets down the knife and steps around the counter to me. "But suicide, suicide I get."

And it clicks.

She hadn't understood. She hadn't understood the clinic, the doctor visits, the times I texted her to pick me up from high school. She hadn't understood whenever the brain fog overtook my thoughts, hadn't understood whenever I refused invitations to connect because the roaring in my head was too much.

Pain is a framework she doesn't understand. But using

that word, *suicide*, put my experience in a framework she recognized. Mental illness is no stranger to suicide. And, due to my family history and my sister, she has had plenty of experience with mental illness. I just needed the right framework to reach her.

I open my arms and let her step into them, knife and all. Her hands have the sharp sting of onion. I don't care. I continue hugging her until the dredges of my coffee go cold.

67

I love, and hate, how long a watercolor painting takes to create.

First, you find a reference or an idea. If I'm working from a photo, I spend a good half hour deciding what elements I want to keep and what to dump, translating the clear pixels to watercolor strokes in my head so there's balance, vibrant colors, thoughtful framing. If I'm working from a sketch, I spend another couple days thinking about the light source and making sure it looks good in a mini-rendering.

Next you're supposed to stretch the paper. Most of the time, I don't bother soaking, stretching, and stapling the substrate flat. I *like* the texture and the sizing, which is the layer of chemicals companies put on the paper. I *like* how the edges curl mid-process. Curling paper is more like a friend, responding to the weight I've burdened it with. Though, lately I've been taping the paper to a board so I can tilt it and create more water movement.

Then comes sketching. The better artist I become, the less sketching I need to do. Fewer lines force me to paint more loosely, which forces me to use my brain and instincts more. The painting looks fresher, deviating from the reference to make the painting *mine.* But I can't jump in without some sort of plan. Once you paint over the white paper, the vibrancy is gone forever, even if you do manage to scrub the white back to life.

Also, putting in a ton of work and then realizing the painting is off-balance with no true light source really sucks.

I pull a scrap paper from a "trash" pile and test colors. Are they friends? Do they play well? Does this shade of sap translate the green in my head? The more frequently I paint, the less I need to test, because I know my paints so well. I even like the risk of introducing a rogue color. Failing forces me to be more creative.

All of this, and I haven't even started *painting*.

The first time you use your brush, you normally start with a light wash. More water than pigment, painting in a roadmap of your destination. And then, you wait for the paint to dry until you can paint on the next layer.

Literally, you're watching paint dry.

I like the waiting.

At this point in a class, I might begin the entire starting process on another painting so I'm not sitting there twiddling my thumbs. I might put my palm across the paper. If it's still cool, the paper isn't truly dry. If I start painting now, I'll create water blossoms. Sometimes I want this effect. Sometimes I don't.

I might lean deeper into my seat and settle into my body again, blink back the pain. I might stand and pace through the wait and the impatience and the pain and watch the other students in their creative flow. What colors do they gravitate toward? What material? What do they think is beautiful? What do they do in the waiting?

The waiting forces me to slow and to take a breath.

If impatience still gnaws, I have space to ask myself: Why? Why do I need to hurry? What is going on inside me that makes me want to be done so fast? Is there something in my life that is pushing me? Is it simply pain? More?

I can tell, deep down, waiting is a really good exercise for me.

I might press my palm across the paper again, lightly. This time the paper might be room temperature. Maybe the pain will lessen a bit too.

Then I paint the next layer and wait again.

68

Whenever Apollo and Athena don't get enough exercise, they roll around on the lounge chair like demons needing to be exorcised, this moaning noise seeping from their throats and the whites of their eyes on full display. *Mom, take the hint and walk us already.*

I rise early from a nap to keep their boredom demon at bay and spend forty minutes with them at the local park. The stress in my legs is a good ache and the cool breeze on my cheeks soothes. I can easily remember the times I spent running alone in nature and the refreshing sensation of hitting an inner limit.

I return home, and, of course, my head is a little aggravated. It's been two and a half years since the clinic, and receiving the right treatment combined with living within my limits along with everything else means I no longer feel as though I'm dying every day. I could quickly cram my writing hours in and call my work finished for the day, but the head aggravation is attached to a string. One quick tug, and my entire brain will unravel. Instead, I eat a slow lunch while I wait for my head to calm enough to write.

An hour and a half later I can journal a paragraph. The next thirty minutes are spent re-waiting for my brain to calm. Another hour passes, and my brain *still* isn't calm enough to work. When can I stop waiting and get on with my life?

When we share the story of our lives, we usually list all the events we waited for. The book deal. The painting sale. The promotion. We say these events make our lives.

Except these events only last a moment. A birth and wedding last less than a day. A second to sign a contract. Then we move onto waiting for the next event.

The truth is, most of our life is spent, not in the events, but in the waiting. Our life is spent in the in-between stage. All those events we wait for? We can't control them. Yet we insist on defining our lives on the very events we can't control.

What if, instead, we consider our lives to be the waiting period, not the event? What we decide to do in the in-between times determine how we spend our lives. Not only would we suddenly have more control over our lives, but we would be less worried about what we can't control.

My life is not whenever the literary agent decides to return my email. My life is not whenever the pain treads more lightly. My life is not six months from now when I can receive the new CGRP medication. My life is not whenever my friend decides to call me.

My life is now, as I'm choosing not to write to take better care of my body.

While I live in the waiting, the mundane becomes valuable. Tiny moments are as weighted and as valuable as the biggest Hollywood event.

I think that's a better way to live.

REPEAT

The cycle repeats *ad infinitum.*

Now I'm ready to create again.

Revelation 21:5a
"Then He who sat on the throne said, 'Behold, I make all things new.'"

69

I'm not known for wearing deep emotions for the world to see. My best friends joke I'm part robot since compartmentalizing is my superpower. I developed the skill as a kid, and migraine was my training ground.

The last time I truly cried was near three years ago, when I left the clinic to face broken china pieces and a life that hadn't changed. But today I cry in Dr. Path's office. The sobbing rushes forward, and I try desperately to shove it back and save the emotions until I'm in a quiet, safe place. The tears still leak through. The nurse tells me the CGRP antibody treatment will be available, not at the end of the year like I'd been told, but next month.

And she can schedule me today.

I clasp my hands over my eyes to keep the liquid in. I'm so, so tired of being in pain, of having my language stolen, of watching my memories fade, of hiding from the light, of letting my body become restless because if I move too much it will aggravate the pain, and yet I need to move. So tired of choosing between my dreams and health.

For a split second, I start dreaming yet again.

Dreaming of the runs I will enjoy. Dreaming of the stories I will write. Dreaming of having kids and attending their plays and soccer games. Dreaming of falling asleep without the ever-accompanying *throb throb throb.*

At home, I rush into our shared office and nudge Randy until he sets aside his schoolwork on his Target desk. After all the highs and lows, all the "no's" from interviews, the course with a life coach, we've figured out the perfect job for him: Counselor. He's back in grad school and loves all his classes. For the first time, he reads as much of his textbooks as he can. He holds my hand as my heart rate speeds up with excitement. *What if, what if, what if?*

"Don't get too excited yet, baby. We need to do more research."

I ride the wave of joy, of heartache as I focus back on reality. Knowing this lottery ticket has a slight chance of winning a million bucks—that I could walk away pain-free—yet focusing on the two bucks it's guaranteed to add—that my pain will most likely reduce a little in severity—feels like a loss.

On the other hand, maybe, *maybe.*

My thoughts flip-flop, and I'm unsure what to think. I'm unsure what to feel except the special numbness that comes with waiting. Who will I be without pain? Will I lose my sense of self? Will I even be the same person? What is my life supposed to look like? What if nothing changes at all?

69

It's enough to drive anyone crazy. And I still have four weeks to wait.

I spend the rest of the morning curled on my favorite chair with Apollo's head on my shin. Deep breathing is the only thing on my agenda for an hour. In the silence, a small voice whispers, "No matter what, I am with you still."

70

Much to my parents' disappointment, my second tattoo stretches about six inches along the backside of my arm. The style is done in a messy calligraphy that scribbles three words: *But if not.*

The phrase comes from the story of Shadrach, Meshach, and Abednego. Despite the Irish trio sounding names, these were three Israeli eunuchs torn from their homeland and forced to live in Babylon under an egotistical king.

Their story basically goes like this:

> King: Bow to my massive, shiny, gold statue! It's of me! And I'm pretty!
>
> Three eunuchs: No.
>
> King: I spent tons of dolla dolla bill!!
>
> Three eunuchs: Still no.

King: Then I'll barbecue you! Look
at the flames on my BBQ cooker!
Three eunuchs: Well, God could
save us, but if not, all's good. So
still a no.
King: Whatevs. *tosses them in*
Then, plot twist: *Four* men appear in
the BBQ cooker, not three. And
they're still alive.
King: What the? 1+1+1 = 3, not 4.
Pull them out!
Three eunuchs: Alive and smoke
free. Look, God saved us
after all!
And the fourth dude? Magically
vanishes. He was either Jesus or
an angel. There's speculation.

I've always liked the story. God could save them, but if not, God is still good and they're still good. The phrase has become a mantra for my life. God could use the CGRP antibodies and fix my brain and take away migraine—but if not, I'm going to be okay. I could write another book, have kids, paint something worthwhile, travel like I dreamed. But if not, I will be okay.

But if not reminds me to live openhanded with the type of Zen yogis envy.

However, this last time I hear the story, I notice a couple details I missed before.

The king heats the furnace seven times hotter than the norm before tossing in the eunuch trio. So hot, the guards who toss the men in die. I've never seen a fire so deadly. In the text, in the very next line, the king notices they aren't dead and rushes to open up the furnace to let them out.

I'm no theologian, but doesn't it seem like there's a time hop?

Physics won't let a furnace turn from *instantly killing all who step within its heat range* to being cool enough to let somebody open the door within the span of a sentence. There's some sort of time lapse.

I don't know how furnaces were built back in the 'ole days. I don't know if the furnace was just a fancy pit of flames or a crème de la crème of kitchen appliances. I do know heat from a fire takes a long time to cool.

Shoot, if I were the king's guards and just saw my buddies fried, I'd probably wait until the fire completely died and there was nothing but ashes before going near the door.

My point is, I always thought the scariest thing about this story was not knowing if the trio were going to be killed or not. I've changed my mind. I think the scariest thing is not knowing how long they sat in the fire.

Some fires rage for hours. Some fires rage for days. Some for weeks.

Did they feel the flames? Feel the scorching heat for days on end? Sure, they walked out fine, but there's just no way to tell what they endured.

It makes me question: How long am I called to this fire? Maybe the CGRP antibodies will work and I will turn out to be a super responder and my pain will be gone forever. Maybe the CGRP antibodies will work a little bit and my flames will cool, going from seven times as hot to four times. Maybe nothing will change. Maybe I'll be asked to live with this in some form for the rest of my life. I don't know. There's no way to tell.

What is comforting is the presence of the fourth man. The text never says how long he stayed with the trio, but I like to think he stayed the entire time. Even if the furnace was a next-sentence type of release, even if the flames went on for hours or days or weeks, the angel or Jesus Himself stayed with them. I like to think it's Jesus. Because He's the one who suffers and experiences pain with us.

As I prepare to go in for my doctor's appointment, I'm trying to hold the outcome with open hands.

The CGRP meds could work for me.

But if not, I'll be okay.

71

I'm afraid to go into the garden. I'm afraid all I'll find is concrete washed by rain and time . . . and nothing else. So this time I bring Apollo.

In real life he is curled over my feet, head resting upon my shin. In my mind, he is by my side, and I thread my fingers through his soft coat. The concrete is still there, but so is the iron fence. Beyond it are smudges of green. I breathe in relief. *I didn't ruin it, then.*

Apollo sniffs the bottom of the fence and looks up at me. The gray of the sky is reflected in his large brown eyes. I think he knows what's going on.

"Come on, boy," I say. The gate, as usual, is unlocked. It creaks with disuse but opens.

The edges of the pebble path are still there, though it needs a fresh layer of stones. Most of the plants have run wild. Ivy swallows the snapdragons, those that aren't already dead. And the trees are sparse, though they still have some leaves.

It's in better condition that I expected. Really, I'm grateful there's anything left.

Apollo sniffs the bushes with glee. His butt wiggles as he dashes from drippy tree to drippy tree, nose shoved into the dead leaves on the ground and the new growth beneath that. I can't help but laugh at his pure joy. The sound soaks into the garden, like water in thirsty soil.

It's time, I think. I whistle at Apollo, who investigates a rabbit hole several yards away. "This way, buddy."

Together we approach the bench.

My heart beats rapidly, a wild creature inside my ribcage. The bench is overgrown with dried vines, but—I grasp toward Apollo to anchor myself—

There He is.

I suck in a breath. *He's here. He's truly here.*

Jesus slides forward on the bench, opening His arms. Apollo doesn't need to be called. He bounds forward, filling those arms with his warm body. Jesus gives him a good scratch behind the ears and underneath the chin, Apollo's favorite spot, but it's as though that isn't close enough for the pup. He climbs into Jesus's lap, somehow fitting all sixty-five pounds of him comfortably into the space. He rubs his head against Jesus's ribs, where the hole once spilled blood and water.

It brings a soft smile to my face.

I slowly sit on the bench, my boots crunching on dead leaves, and take one of Apollo's dangling ears between my fingers to rub. He wears a sleepy grin on his face, eyes rolled back in contentment. I don't dare look at Jesus. I'm afraid of what I'll find.

"There's no fear here." His voice holds no ill will toward me, no grudge, no hint of anger. It is pure light.

My chest traps my breath—and I turn to look.

His features are clearer now. His smile is warm and wrinkly. His hazel eyes sparkle with the same kindness that soaks Randy's gaze. It's forgiveness. It's understanding.

It's love.

Tears prick the back of my eyes, but I can't pinpoint why.

I want to come closer to Him, to melt into the kindness, but it's insurmountable. I don't know how to bridge the gap, to merge cell upon cell until we are no longer two people but one. The want burns like a smoldering fire.

Finally, I choke out, "I don't know how to love You."

Jesus continues to stroke Apollo. The silence isn't awkward, just true. He flips over His wrists, and I see the stigmata. "That's okay. Because I know how to love you."

I wave to the space between us. "But I don't know how to *know* You."

He leans over and hugs me, pulling me into Him. He smells like autumn and joy. And hope. "That's okay too. Because *I* know you. And that's all that really matters."

We sit in the budding garden a long, long time, holding Apollo while he sleeps.

72

The day is bright and sunny with the clear cerulean skies Coloradans adore. My leg is still sore from the CGRP shot I finally took last week. I have a reaction, and the injection site is tender and swollen to the size of my palm and a pissed-off pink. Antihistamines seem to help. It turns out I am not one of the patients who receives immediate relief, which means I'll have to wait for several months to see just how much I respond to the CGRP antibodies. The river is burbling next to me, and the walking path isn't yet busy. It's a perfect morning. Not just because the weather is heavenly, but because Anna is smiling.

A true, soul-reaching smile.

She waddles next to me as we walk our dogs. Her baby is five months on the way, and, for some magical reason, pregnancy has been wonderful for her mood. She's the most stable she's been in years. It's like she's colored in; all the pieces of herself are present and vibrant.

We walk with Starbucks in hand, and I listen as she describes her nursery decorations. They are going with a Star Wars theme since her husband is a massive fan. I make a mental note to incorporate stars into her baby shower.

Her book hasn't been published, yet. But it also doesn't need to be. She's more herself than she has ever been. And it's wonderful, like I finally got my sister back.

It's strange, how much illness has stolen from us. It's also strange how much it has given.

If I had been healthy, I would've continued working for Sarah. I would've gone to grad school. Would've had children on autopilot because that's what you do after you get married. Would've joined the rat race of life without putting any thought into why.

Instead, I've been able to carve out a corner of the world for myself. I can write and create, which is what truly fits me. I am forced to weigh and consider everything, so nothing is on autopilot and the work I do is thoughtful and intentional. I dream of having children, but relish the freedom I currently have, and if/when I do have them, I am more certain to be present for each moment.

I have been given presence and patience and an appreciative eye for small bits of beauty. The swirl of a bath bomb into the drain. The way music drifts through an empty house during a silent night when pain keeps me awake. The taste of a well-savored cup of tea. The art of making a house a home.

I have time to be, to spend in my garden, both metaphysical and not.

72

I can breathe.
I soak up Anna's happiness as though it is my own.

73

I think a lot more about people in the Bible who experienced healing miracles. Specifically, the woman who touched Jesus's robe. During this time, whenever a woman had menstrual bleeding, she was considered unclean and had to live apart from her community. This particular woman spent twelve years being ostracized by her people. Twelve years living apart because of her unstoppable, continuous bleeding. *Twelve* years.

I keep thinking about how often we expect miracles to happen whenever we pray. We never talk about Paul, who prayed three times and then considered no longer praying. As far as we know, he was never healed from this mysterious "thorn in his side." We certainly never talk about the woman who bled for twelve years before she found healing. And we definitely don't talk about what to do when there is no healing at all.

I've had prayer spoken over me. I've had hands laid on

me. I've had one person pray at a time. I've had almost thirty people pray at a single time. I've been anointed with oil. I've taken special communion. I've had demonic intervention. I've had pretty much every spiritual tactic applied to me, and still God has not said yes.

For most of my life, I never expected God to heal me. This year is the first time I wondered if I might be like the woman who bled for twelve years. Maybe I'll only have to go through this pain for a certain amount of time. For so long, my life has been about survival, then finding emotional contentment, but maybe this year God is going to physically heal me. For a disease like migraine, which has no cure and is severely underfunded, it isn't very likely physical healing will come entirely from Western medicine.

I start wondering this, not just because the story popped in my mind again, but because after taking the CGRP treatment for two years, my migraine changed slightly. The mysterious mix of major lifestyle change and management, other coping mechanisms, the right medication, treating vasospasm, and no more Botox shifts the scale. I now have days that aren't filled with severe pain. My abortives work better half the time. Coffee dates appear on my calendar again. Word counts accumulate. My to-do list gets checked off regularly. Shoot, I even *have* a to-do list.

Of course, I still have to manage the pain. But it's a shift. It's slightly better.

It's frightening.

There's another story of healing in Scripture, where Jesus asked the sick man by the pool of Bethesda, "Do you want to be well?" I'm tempted to scream, *What type of stupid question is* that? *Of* course *he wants to be well. Nobody wants to be in pain. Nobody wants to be sick.*

However, I find myself asking this same question: Do I want to get well?

Answering with anything other than "Yes!" is utterly stupid, but it doesn't seem as simple as a three-letter word.

Getting well means facing an entirely new unknown. Getting well means facing an entirely new identity. When the pain came, I had to learn who I was without the friends, without the extroverted nature, without the high energy. I had to get to know this quieter, more sensitive version of me.

To have an inkling of my old self return again? I don't know that person. I don't know her, and I certainly don't know if I *want* to be her. I like my new self. I've reached peace. I actually enjoy me. I'm afraid I won't recognize the person in the mirror.

In a similar vein: What if I don't *like* this new version of my old self? She has no idea how to be an adult, since she turned chronic as a teen. She doesn't know how to be married or how to do taxes or how to hold deep friendship.

Yes, God, I do want to get well. But this freaking scares me. I'm scared to see who I am. I'm scared, because I don't know who I am.

If this slightly better doesn't last, so be it. I'm used to what I know.

If this slightly better does last, I have a feeling we'll be figuring out who I am together.

74

The next time I enter the garden, I make a pitstop first.

I imagine an isolated island with a crater in the middle of it, not unlike a blown volcano. The pit smokes as though the explosion had been recent. The sides are caked with lava rock, molten smooth and slippery, which makes it near impossible to climb. The entire thing is ink-black, though lines of vibrant crimson from still-smoldering fire crack across its length like splinters.

I'm gasping from the effort, and my mouth is dust dry from lack of water. But eventually, eventually, I grasp the waving ridge of the top.

I haul myself up, knees scratching as they find purchase, and peer over the edge.

Inside the crater is a whirling tangle of slate gray smoke. As I watch, a blessed breeze blows through and sweeps the mess away.

I can finally see into the depths.

There—at the very bottom—

Is a girl.

I heave myself higher, letting the ledge cut into my stomach to see better. She's curled into a fetal position as though the entire mountain had been pressed upon her and it was all she could do to save herself. The edges of her are scarlet, and I realize she's still burning.

She never stopped.

Her hair is a soft blonde-brown, though it's matted with dirt. Her skin white. Her legs long, torso short. Her eyes fly open, and they are a mix of blue and gold, appearing green in the distance. Like mine.

Oh.

She's me.

"Hello down there!" I call. My voice echoes inside the crater like a ball rattling around an empty can.

The girl lifts her head. Blinks at the sun, as though she hasn't seen light in a very, very long time. "Hello?" Her voice is rusty from disuse. She seems surprised to be alive. She tries to move her arms, but they are stiff, and when she leans on them, they fold beneath her weight. She stretches out her legs instead, her joints slow and creaky.

"What's your name?" I ask.

The girl is on her knees now. She reels a bit, as though this movement is almost too much. She places a hand to her head and pauses, feeling, waiting. "I . . . I don't remember."

"It's Abby," I say. "It's nice to meet you."

She tries to stand, but her legs still don't support her. She flops back to the ground. "You too," she says. But then she bows her head, as though the distance between us is too much for her to handle. I guess I look impossibly high from up here.

I reach a hand, it extends further and further, to a distance not humanly possible, until it dangles in front of her.

She doesn't look. Turns her head to the slick joint where the crater wall meets the floor.

I brush her cheek. A small, *you can do it* motion.

Her arm rises as though it's a balloon, like it can't help but take flight, as though it's coded into its very nature. Her hand catches in mine. Her palm burns, but it matches the burning in me.

Because I have never stopped burning either.

I heave, leaning back, and I help tug her out of the pit and into the light.

75

When you write a book, you build that book layer by layer. First you start with the zero draft, then you build the first draft and the book's bones. Round after round of edits nails the true skeleton. Add muscles and skin through the finesse of sentences. Add a sparkle of freckles last.

Like painting, the magic lies in the layers.

Unfortunately, sometimes the layers never seem to end.

I'm finishing yet another round of revisions, trying to create a story that makes sense. Every time I get closer to finishing, I find another layer of edits to complete. I circle back to each layer until I'm ready to throw my laptop out the window. Eventually, you have to say *good enough* and let it go. Otherwise, I'll spend my entire life tinkering and never move on to the next project.

I spend years trying to form a theology that can support my pain. For a while, my framework for life works. Another plot twist happens or my pain medicine reacts in a way I don't expect or I become sick on top of being sick, which is an entirely different level of hell.

Then the framework no longer fits. I'm forced to tear myself open to the bones to try to figure out a better way to support my life and pain. I keep returning, revising and revising and revising.

Eventually, I have to say *good enough* and live with my framework, even if it's not complete. Will I ever truly be finished tinkering with my theology, with my framework, with a skeleton that holds me up? Probably not. Absolutely not. That doesn't mean I should stop living.

When creating, at some point I'll also have to decide on the meaning of my work. Will this series truly be about losing dreams? Will it be about family relationships? About loss? Or will my main character charge in a completely new direction? Will this painting be a commentary on social justice or the simple beauty of a flower?

Did this meaning organically rise from the creation? Or do I, as the artist, create meaning and guide my creation into the vision I had?

Or does my creation have meaning despite whatever I say? That just by existing, it has value and meaning beyond myself?

I can ask these same questions of my life. Does my meaning organically rise from the shape of my life? Does my pain naturally give my life a certain theme? Can I build a life around my pain to give it a certain type of meaning based on my vision? Or, just from my very existence, do I have value and meaning? God created me and loves me. I exist and therefore I have meaning, even if I never find out what it is.

76

I'm stretching out my thigh from yet another monthly CGRP shot when I find the canvas leaning in the hallway.

"Babe?" I call out. "What's this?"

It's no painting I did, that's for sure. The frame has been smashed and the canvas itself has been stabbed and shredded. It barely holds together. One wrong tug will tear it apart. And the broken, slashed word written across it?

HOPE.

Randy jogs out of our bedroom. He's looking sharp in gray pants and a cerulean plaid. His military cut has grown out a bit and is styled back.

"Oh, that's my painting for group." He's currently leading a counseling group for mental health, for both those with mental illness and their loved ones. He dashes into his workshop. "We're talking about anger and grief," he says, muffled. "I'm bringing in my art."

I pick up the frame. It nearly falls apart in my hands. "Seems a little . . . I dunno. Dark?"

He reemerges with his whip-like painting and props the canvas against the wall so he won't forget it. "That's 'cause it's not done." He plucks the beaten canvas from my hands and retreats again into his workshop.

I catch a glimpse of the finished project as he's leaving. He added scarlet thread, stitching the canvas back together from the bottom to the top. The word HOPE is whole again.

It's perfect.

77

I recently read the book *Silence* by Shūsaku Endō, which takes place in the 1600s during the Tokugawa shogunate, the Japanese feudal military government in the Edo period.

When the Japanese government decided to create fumi-e, they hired a local artist. Each fumi-e was not unlike a stepping stone, stamped with important images from Christianity, like the persecution and the crucifixion and the resurrection and the virgin birth. The shogunate, rulers appointed by the Emperor, would then force Christians to step on these fumi-e as an act of apostatizing.

The artist did such a great job on the fumi-e when he gave them over to the government officials, they looked at each other and said, "These have so much emotion nobody could have created these unless they themselves were Christian."

They went back to the artist and asked him if he was a Christian. Turns out, when he had started creating the fumi-e, he was not. But through the process of creating and contemplating Christ on the cross, he became one. And they killed him for it.

I'm not sure if this artist story is true or not. I searched for a while but couldn't find any real evidence. But I hope it is.

How beautiful: to create work so transcendental anybody can see truth written in it. To create work so emotional, one glance would reveal the creator's faith.

I relate to Rodriguez, the missionary who came to Japan with visions in his head of what martyrdom and suffering looks like. He expected to die for his faith. I remember flipping through Foxe's *Book of Martyrs* as a child, wondering if I would ever be strong enough to withstand that sort of suffering.

But as I read, I saw Rodriguez question his faith, question God's silence about the Japanese people's pain. Especially as he realized his suffering was not what he expected. Instead of being faced with death, the government officials gave him a choice: They would end the torture of his fellow Christians if he rejected Christ and stepped on the fumi-e.

He chose to deny Christ and step.

Rodriguez believed he would die in a blaze of glory holding his faith. Instead, he died alone in Japan, excommunicated from the church and forever branded with shame because he decided to apostate, to deny Jesus, to save others from pain.

Some say Rodriguez made a mistake in apostatizing to save others. Denying Jesus is a massive no-no in the church.

One of the worst things you can possibly do. Living the rest of his life isolated in Japan was confirmation of Rodriguez's mistake.

I disagree.

When Rodriguez apostatized, it was a perfect picture of the gospel. He gave up his own glory, dreams, and pride to save somebody else. Christ came to be stepped on, to be sacrificed. That's the entire point of the cross. Even though Rodriguez outwardly denied Christ, he could not have acted more Christ-like.

Yet from the outside, everyone looked at Rodriguez and judged him. His church back in Spain seethed with disappointment. When he stepped, only he knew he walked in faith. After everything Rodriguez went through, he came out different. So did his relationship with God. He now knew God in an entirely different way.

I've asked the same questions as Rodriguez. I *still* ask those same questions.

I, too, have been surprised at the shape of pain.

Sometimes I wonder if others think I have apostatized. Because I question and I lament and I stopped attending church in lieu of listening to sermons online because I'd rather not aggravate my brain by sitting through a service. Because I do not volunteer and have chosen to leave the pithy sayings and other "marks of being a good Christian" behind.

Then I wonder if the others who do these things with certainty will judge me because shouldn't I be more certain in my beliefs? Sometimes I'd rather be like Rodriquez and be forced to leave community behind. But there is value in community, even in a broken one, and I cannot in good conscience step fully away.

My relationship with God now is different. I'm different. It's not less or more valuable, not less or more earnest, not less or more heartfelt, not less or more stumbling through the dark trying to follow Christ's light.

Just different.

78

Several of the migraine communities I'm a part of start advertising for an upcoming documentary called *Out of My Head*. I click through and find it's playing in a nearby theater. Randy and I invite my parents, and they sit next to us during the showing. I feel extremely loved that they would willingly spend thirty bucks to come watch a movie for me.

At first, the movie is extremely hard to watch. Depictions of auras the size of a house, the variations and patterns and colors and flickering lights triggers my nausea. Even hearing the word *migraine* in a booming voice is enough to send my world spinning. I've never heard the word so big and so large. It's the first time the portrayal of the word matches my experience of it. The first time I've ever seen a migraine on a screen portrayed as a disability and not as a joke.

Funny thing is, watching the migraine documentary spikes my migraine pain. That night I can't sleep without having Cefaly pinned to my forehead. Even then, every time the device quits, the pain wakes me up, and I have to turn it on again just to get some shut-eye.

I love how the documentary shows various artists and writers who struggle with migraine. The screen fills with excerpts of work and paintings. A lot of these artists make sense of their suffering through their art. The documentary points out a lot of similarities between Lewis Carroll and Alice's experiences in Wonderland, which are eerily similar to aspects of migraine. Personally, I find Carroll's work to be so whacked I've never been able to finish it. I can only stomach the Disney and canceled *Once Upon a Time* versions.

My favorite portrayed artist is Hildegard of Bingen, a medieval Benedictine abbess with a gift for writing and composing. She had all the stages typical of a migraine but attributed them to God. Her spiritual experiences are described as similar to the euphoria stage.

This frightens me.

I don't know if some of my spiritual experiences are a byproduct of my disease. That, if they are tied to migraine, they will be negated.

Maybe, in the end, where they come from doesn't matter. They're still part of my story.

But I like what the documentary concludes about her—by creating, Hildegard gained some mastery over her pain.

Like my attempt at painting an aura, these words are my way of gaining some mastery over my pain. To create good, to create hope. To pour words and hold them and my life and my questions with open hands, like I cradle a still-wet watercolor painting. To read a character arc between jagged lines of questions and auras and throbbing pain. To paint meaning, not because pain itself has meaning, but because meaning exists despite it. To trace the tension between art and God and pain and press on the quivering nerve until the muscle relaxes. To continue on, despite still being afraid.

I don't know if the CGRP antibody treatments will work more than they already have. They might. They might not. I may be creative because of my disease or in spite of my disease or a bit of both. I don't know. I don't think it matters. Because I'm still here.

I'm still here.

AUTHOR'S NOTE

As of writing this paragraph, I have had four years of the CGRP antibody treatment. After tweaking some treatments and adding in others, I have found more improvement. I can enjoy long walks along the riverside and spend hours binge reading a good book. I can enjoy an afternoon-long date with my husband and dream again of the future. There is still migraine and pain, but I have days now where the pain is mild. It feels life-changing.

ACKNOWLEDGEMENTS

Life is both far longer and far shorter than it seems, and it means a lot that you would spend some of yours with me. Thank you. I hope you found something here that resonates.

Also, a quick thank you to my parents, especially my mom.

Anna, your time and insight and encouragement.

Randy, always.

But I tell you this often.

Another quick thanks to Anita, my editor, for her wisdom.

Colleen and the other painters at the studio, for teaching me how to paint and listen and for being a source of true joy.

The Queens of the Quill and Kate for continued support.

My doctors and counselors.

And Apollo and Athena, for their unconditional love and motivation to get off my butt and move.

ALSO BY ABBY J. REED

Fiction:

When Planets Fall

(Sirkel Galaxy #1)

When Dreamers Fall

(Sirkel Galaxy #2)

When Royals Fall

(Sirkel Galaxy #3)

When Heroes Fall

(Sirkel Galaxy #4)

Spotlight

(Light Galaxy #1)

Darklight

(Light Galaxy #2)

Limelight

(Light Galaxy #3)

Newlight

(Light Galaxy #4)

ABOUT THE AUTHOR

Abby J. Reed is the author of the LIGHT GALAXY and SIRKEL GALAXY series and the nonfiction book, THE COLOR OF PAIN. She has a degree in English Writing, a certificate in Spiritual Formation from Denver Seminary, and is drawn to characters with physical limitations due to her own neurological disorder called Chronic Migraine.

Abby lives in Colorado with her family and fluffy gremlin. If her hands aren't on the keyboard, they are stained purple and blue with paint. Find her online at www.abbyjreed.com.

www.ingramcontent.com/pod-product-compliance
Ingram Content Group UK Ltd.
Pitfield, Milton Keynes, MK11 3LW, UK
UKHW020419250726
13967UKWH00007B/2718

9 781953 615060